GUIDE TO
CRANKBAITS AND JERKBAITS

CHOOSING AND USING
DIVING BAITS FOR BASS

MONTGOMERY, ALABAMA

INTRODUCTION
Making Crankbaits Your First Choice

THE CRANKBAIT is the one lure found inside the tacklebox that too often gets a bum wrap. Correct usage does not require the experience needed to deftly flip or pitch a jig or worm into tight quarters. Similarly, the dexterity required to work magic with a topwater lure is not necessary to entice a strike.

Fundamentally, all it takes to make a crankbait work is a blind cast and a monotonous retrieve. As a result, the simple mechanics required to fish with a crankbait sometimes stereotype it as a lure for novice anglers.

But experienced bass fishermen know better. More than once in this encyclopedia of cranking, you will find the names of David Fritts and Mark Davis, whose early successes were achieved by using lipped lures.

Through the shared wisdom of Fritts, Davis and other experts, this book will dispel the misleading notion that crankbaits are for beginners. And it will also reveal a few very unorthodox applications for lipped baits, including Carolina rigging and fishing lipped baits designed for deep water in the shallows.

Indeed, as the skill level of anglers continues to increase, so do the newfound applications for crankbaits. And this continuing transformation has taken place in a relatively short period when compared to the modern revolution of bass fishing that began when BASS was established in the late 1960s.

One of the first modern crankbaits recognized by the pros was the "alphabet" series of lures that launched the category as it's known today. The first, carved from wood by Fred Young, was called the Big O. At the time, crankbaits for the most part were made from wood or metal and had elongated, flat bills protruding from their bodies. With trolling illegal in BASS tournaments, the pros were eager to embrace a lipped lure like the Big O, which could be cranked with ease when compared to the arm-numbing strain from winching a Hellbender on a hot summer day.

Crankbaits today come in lifelike patterns that emulate shad and crawfish, two food staples of bass. By design, today's crankbaits will run from just beneath the surface to depths of 25 feet or more.

While the modern crankbait was undergoing its facelift, another revolution was underway with a similar category of lure. The slender floating minnow, made of hard plastic, morphed into what is today called the jerkbait.

Jerkbaits are classified as reaction lures, and rightfully so. The erratic diving, flashing and darting action they impart, oftentimes triggers the predator instinct of the bass, whether or not it's in search of a meal.

Knowing the nuances of jerkbaits and crankbaits, and recognizing that they should have top shelf recognition in the tacklebox, will make you a more rounded bass fisherman. And a more successful angler.

Copyright 2004 by BASS

Published in 2004 by BASS
5845 Carmichael Road
Montgomery, AL 36117

Editor In Chief:
Dave Precht

Editor:
James Hall

Managing Editor:
Craig Lamb

Editorial Assistant:
Althea Goodyear

Art Director:
Rick Reed

Designers:
Laurie Willis, Leah Cochrane,
Bill Gantt, Nancy Lavender

Illustrators:
Chris Armstrong, Shannon Barnes,
Lenny McPherson, Tom Seward

Photography Manager:
Gerald Crawford

Contributing Writers:
Darl Black, Wade Bourne, David Hart,
Mark Hicks, Michael Jones,
Bob McNally, John Neporadny Jr.,
Steve Price, Tom Seward, Louie Stout,
Tim Tucker, Don Wirth

Contributing Photographers:
Chris Altman, Charles Beck, Darl Black,
Wade Bourne, Steve Bowman, Soc Clay,
Gerald Crawford, Tom Evans,
David Hart, Bryan Hendricks,
Mark Hicks, Michael Jones, Craig Lamb,
Bill Lindner, Peter B. Mathiesen,
Bob McNally, John Neporadny Jr.,
Steve Price, David J. Sams, Tom Seward,
Doug Stamm, Louie Stout,
Gary Tramontina, Tim Tucker,
Don Wirth

Copy Editors:
Laura Harris, Debbie Salter

Manufacturing Manager:
Bill Holmes

Marketing:
Betsy B. Peters

**Vice President &
General Manager, BASS:**
Dean Kessel

Printed on American paper by
RR Donnelley

ISBN 1-890280-06-2

CRANKBAITS are the cleanup lures of the tacklebox. They can search for fish, trigger reaction strikes when fishing is slow, and locate habitat and bottom contours, among other useful applications.

CONTENTS

ALL ABOUT CRANKBAITS

A Deceiving Name For

A Versatile Lure …

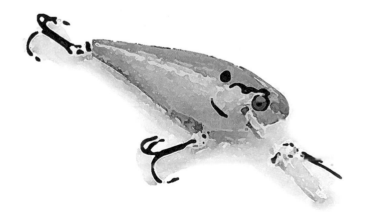

CRANKBAITS: A VERSATILE TOOL

There's a lot more to fishing crankbaits than just chunking and winding

ASK ANY BASS FISHERMAN to pick the top three lures he can't do without, and most likely, crankbaits will be on the list. Just in terms of versatility and big fish potential, the king of the hard baits pretty much sets the standard for anything in its wake.

For most, the real genius of crankbaits is in their simplicity. Even in the hands of novice anglers, crankbaits are relatively easy to use. The mechanics of cast-and-retrieve seem to come rather quickly with baits that are built to do at least part of the work.

However, the seduction of this simplicity comes in that four letter word: w-o-r-k. Work, that is, not in cranking a reel handle, but doing the heavy lifting necessary in finding fish and refining patterns.

While there are methods of shortening the learning curve, noted crankbait expert David Fritts can only laugh at the thought of a simple answer.

"A lot of times, there aren't any criteria for finding them quickly. Like any other kind of fishing, crankbaits require a lot of hard work. But if you need to find fish fast, my theory is to pick a small area of the lake and just fish it. Once I figure out the depth and where the fish are located, I start expanding on the whole lake," says the acknowledged master of the crankbait discipline.

"I like to pick out a major creek on the map — one that looks like it has a lot of structure. In other words, a crooked creek channel that winds from one side to the other, with bends and doglegs. This is the area I want to look at first."

CRANKBAITS WITH long plastic bills will deflect off wood cover and trigger the predator instinct of the bass.

crankbait, your distance from the target area and so on, it's very easy to miss the key spot," observes Mike Auten, a touring pro on the BASS circuit.

"If I see other anglers fishing in the vicinity of my area, I don't let it bother me. Sometimes they don't know how to position their boat correctly to get the right angle. It's all about the angle of attack and moving at a speed where you can accurately identify those key spots."

This concept of finding the "spot within a spot" is at the very core of tournament competition. It is equally important to recreational anglers, who must locate bass on heavily pressured waters. However, this ultimate refinement of the crankbait process only comes after the grunt work of locating productive areas.

THE NEED FOR SPEED

At first glance, the tremendous advantage of crankbaits — aside from their proven action — is the speed in which they can be used. If the term "run and gun" had been coined with any bass technique in mind, it could very easily have been crankbaits.

"Speed is fine if you know exactly where the spots are located, but far too many people get going too fast. With so many variables involved in how your boat is positioned, the running depth of the

Crankbait Tips

Metal-lipped crankbaits are considered antique lures when compared to today's flashy models. And that is precisely why they are deadly now. The fish are not accustomed to hearing and seeing their wide wobble and unique action. What is more, they are the most weedless crankbaits in the category.

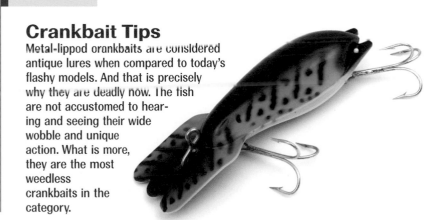

Searching For Answers

When using crankbaits as search tools, one of the toughest decisions is how long to stay in any given area. Move too fast, and miss the bite. Move too slowly, and waste valuable time. For crankbait guru David Fritts, the answers come easier at those moments when he knows that an area holds a fish.

This is the moment when he can learn precisely how the fish wants the bait presented.

"One of the keys to being a better crankbait fisherman is learning how the fish want that bait. If there is a fish in a certain area, the whole deal is figuring out what to do to make that fish bite it.

"If I know there is a fish in an area, I give it at least 30 to 40 minutes. And I'll fish the lure differently on every cast until I figure out exactly how that fish wants it. Then, I know how to fish the rest of the lake."

FRITTS BELIEVES patience is the key when using crankbaits as search tools.

ELIMINATION FACTOR

To Fritts, the real speed advantage of crankbaits is in their ability to eliminate water quickly. This sometimes tedious process should not be confused with actually catching fish. Quite often, the best crankbait fishermen in the world spend days not setting the hook, and that doesn't seem to bother them.

"When I fish for half a day without catching anything, I don't look at it as being bad, or that the fish aren't biting a crankbait. I've just eliminated water and need to keep doing something different, fishing different depths until I find the fish. It's unfortunate, but usually when I'm looking for fish, it takes more than a day to figure out how to catch them. I'm eliminating water and getting a little wiser. Believe it or not, I've won tournaments when I practiced for three days without catching a fish," notes Fritts.

THE AMBUSH POINT

Once this trial-and-error method has produced some likely areas and, most importantly, the key fish-holding depth, the spot-in-spot process begins in earnest.

"Remember, all the really obvious stuff stands out to other fishermen. These places are hard to find, because you have to drop the trolling motor and just fish," reminds Auten.

"You might fish for 100 yards and not get a bite. You just keep on fishing. To me, sometimes it's getting on a long river ledge, not fishing the junctions, but just looking for irregular spots along that ledge, places that aren't on the map. These are where the fish will be, but they're not the obvious spots."

These small, key spots are what Fritts calls "ambush points," places where bass come to feed. They may all live in the general area, but this is where they meet up at mealtime. More importantly, they are almost always in the zone where the shallowest water meets the deepest water. If a stump, rock or other object is positioned on that precise spot, it will invariably produce fish.

The consistency of these areas is linked to a number of factors, including seasonal patterns, bait, weather, water fluctuations and fishing pressure. Whether the fish will be there from one day to the next is difficult to forecast, and experience goes a long way in making an educated guess.

"I can get a fairly good idea when I get a bite in practice. You get a bite for a reason. Bass are really pretty simple once you figure them out — they are usually near the place where you caught a fish the day before, so you stand a good chance of catching another one," observes Fritts.

"They're living there for some reason. The bait is there, or the oxygen level is right — there is some reason."

THE MILK RUN

To shift the percentages in an angler's favor, the work ethic of crankbait fishing pays big dividends to those who can find multiple areas. In building a "milk run" of likely places, a fisherman can then take advantage of the one thing that many others overlook: timing.

By simply returning to areas at critical times, it is quite possible to be more productive in a very short amount of time. While changes in water and weather conditions can alter or perhaps short-circuit the daily feeding cycles, it is a crucial part of crankbait strategy upon which pros like Fritts rely.

"From years and years of my fishing experience, I've discovered that if you find bass at a certain time, the bite will be an hour later every day. It sounds strange, but I've found it to be true more times than not."

But no matter how carefully an angler selects his spots, determines the correct depth range, times his fishing day and makes the perfect casts, it can all come to a bad end if he doesn't have an intimate knowledge of the tools being used. To be specific, an angler must know the precise depth that every crankbait in his box will reach.

Maintaining Cranking Depths

It is important to note, says David Fritts, that crankbaits will not reach their maximum depth until the lure is about three-quarters of the way back to the boat. Moreover, it is quite possible to test five identical baits and have all five run at different depths. A notation of the depth — made with a waterproof marker under the bill — is the final step.

Of course, it is imperative that these depth tests be done with the same line-test (10-pound line would be a good choice), so there is a consistent frame of reference. Since angling conditions change, as do the line-tests required, an angler needs to understand how a different line-test will affect the maximum depth of any crankbait.

"With different line-tests, you'll normally see a change of somewhere between 8 inches to 1 foot of depth for every change in line size. For instance, if

FRITTS USES his rod to make a crankbait run a few feet, either shallower or deeper.

you have a bait that runs 10 feet deep on 10-pound line, changing to 8-pound line will make that bait probably run about a foot deeper, at 11 feet. Now, if you put on 12-pound line, it will run somewhere at 9 feet or a touch above," counsels Fritts.

"The problem comes when you're using 14- or 17-pound test. That really robs you of depth — probably a foot for each pound-test.

"The easiest way to control depth is to stick with a line size you're comfortable with and use your rod to control the depth. If you need to run shallower, hold your rod up. If you need to run at maximum depth, hold the rod tip 1 inch from the water."

CRANKBAITS IN-DEPTH

Know the subtle way to match the right crankbait to the situation

I F YOU CHOOSE CRANKBAITS purely on the basis of running depth or color, you're probably not catching as many bass as you should.

At a glance, crankbait designs and features may seem insignificant, yet even the most subtle characteristic can cause a bass to crush a lure one day and ignore it the next.

"Anglers tend to lump crankbaits in one category," says four time world champion Rick Clunn. "But the truth is, there are some specialized tools within the crankbait families that we must use to appeal to the sensitive awareness of the fish."

The ability to recognize those characteristics and match them to each fishing condition leads to a better lure presentation and a higher success. And while those subtle differences in lures may seem insignificant, they can really matter to the fish.

"We often forget how aware bass are of their environment, or how sharp their attention to details can be when compared to ours," explains Clunn. "Sometimes the subtle differences in a crankbait's performance play a bigger role in catching fish than most anglers realize."

(Opposite page) CRANKBAIT aficionados like Rick Clunn believe in using both plastic and wood baits because each offers distinct strike enticing advantages.

Once you learn to identify each crankbait's features, you'll begin tying on baits that increase your chances of success. Here's a look at crankbait design characteristics and how they relate to fishing situations:

THE QUIRKS OF WOOD AND PLASTIC

Both wood and plastic crankbaits deserve a spot in the tacklebox because of their performance differences. Most wooden baits are more buoyant than plastic, therefore they will rise faster when stopped during the retrieve. Some pros believe

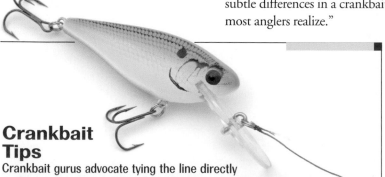

Crankbait Tips

Crankbait gurus advocate tying the line directly to the lure's split ring. Even then, the knot can get caught in the tiny gap where the ends of the wire ring meet and gouge the line, making it weak. To avoid this, always cinch the knot onto the split ring, with the gap halfway between the bait's eye and the knot.

Tackling Crankbaits: Mark Davis

Using the right tackle is critical with diving crankbaits, since tackle plays a determining role in a bait's action and running depth. These things, in turn, contribute to its effectiveness.

"You've got to match your tackle to your lure," Mark Davis says. "To do this, I use two rod-and-reel combinations for diving crankbaits. For bigger baits, I use a 7-foot fiberglass medium action rod and 12- to 14-pound-test line. Or if I'm fishing around snaggy cover such as logs or brush, I may go as heavy as 17- to 20-pound test.

"For smaller baits, I switch to spinning tackle. I designed a 6-foot, 6-inch rod for the Falcon rod company just for this purpose. It has a parabolic action and an oversized stripping guide just up from the reel. This reduces drag from the line on that first guide, and it produces longer, smoother casts." Davis normally spinfishes with 8-pound-test line.

"Spinning tackle allows me to pull smaller baits at the same depths that baitcasters have to use bigger baits to get to," Davis explains. "I know that a nonaggressive fish is a lot more likely to hit a little bait than a big one. This is one secret that's helped me in a lot of tournaments."

wood baits can be more effective for cranking through brush and over weeds because they are less prone to snagging. On the other hand, they say, less buoyant plastic baits are good for cold water, when a slow rising crankbait is desired.

Florida pro Shaw Grigsby believes most wood baits have a more pronounced wobble than plastic lures, making them easier to feel during the retrieve.

"The buoyancy of wood has more deflection capabilities, too," he adds. "So when you're banging it into stumps or rocks, it glances off more suddenly than plastic, and that can trigger more strikes."

There also are differences within the types of wood and plastic used by manufacturers. Most plastic lures are made of either ABS or Butyrate, while wooden lures are carved from balsa.

Butyrate plastic is clear, denser and heavier than ABS, therefore it tends to be used more in transparent or ghost-colored lures or in deep diving crankbaits, where density can enhance castability. And because it is heavier, Butyrate crankbaits are easier to modify as suspending baits than ABS lures. (You can determine the type of plastic used in painted lures by scraping away the paint. If it's bone-colored or a milky plastic, it's probably ABS.)

Although two rattling lures of the same model and similar color may appear to be the same, it's possible that one is made of Butyrate and the other of ABS, offers Storm Lures' Jim Morton. Storm's Magnum Wiggle Warts, for example, may be made of either because some anglers prefer clear lips (made of Butyrate) while others want them painted (ABS).

"If the bass seem to bite one better than the other on a given day, it could be because of the subtle difference in material and not necessarily because of the color of the bill," says Morton. "It could be a slight sound difference, since rattling Butyrate baits produce a

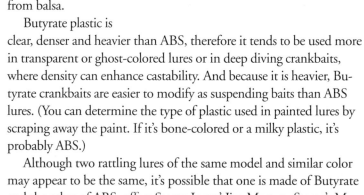

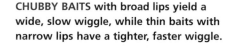

CHUBBY BAITS with broad lips yield a wide, slow wiggle, while thin baits with narrow lips have a tighter, faster wiggle.

duller sound than ABS baits."

There are differences between balsa and cedar wooden baits as well. Balsa is usually lighter and more buoyant than cedar, thus it can produce a livelier wiggle than cedar. Conversely, cedar is denser, so it's easier to cast in a strong wind and rises slower.

When choosing between plastic and wood, remember that wooden crankbaits may vary more widely in performance than plastic lures because of the consistency differences in each piece of wood.

As you might suspect, those natural characteristics of plastic and wood lures are affected by the shape and design of the body and the diving bill.

KEVIN VANDAM favors crankbaits with a tight wiggle in early springtime when fishing cool water.

ACTION AND DEPTH

The crankbait's lip design and the location of the line tie play a major role in how deep the bait runs and whether it has a tight wiggle or a wide wobble. Long, straight lips will dive deeper than short, angled lips. However, the line tie can be an overriding factor in running depth.

"The location of the eyelet onto which you tie the line makes all the difference in the running depth and action a lure will give you," says all star pro Kevin VanDam. "The closer it is to the body of the bait, the deeper it will run and the tighter the wiggle will be. If it's farther out on the end of the bill, it will run shallower and wobble wider. Also, the bills that angle down run shallower and have a wider wobble."

Bill shape affects deflection qualities, too. Squared-off or four-cornered baits deflect more intensely than rounded bills, says Clunn.

"When a rounded bill catches on a limb, it tends to slide off," he explains. "One of the keys to this style of

LIKE THE BAITFISH they imitate, crankbaits are natural choices for fishing around wooden objects. Choose the square-bill models when fishing in heavy cover to avoid frequent hang-ups.

Tackling Crankbaits: Ken Cook

Ken Cook mainly relies on long baitcast rods with diving crankbaits but he differs from Mark Davis and most other pros in one important respect. "Some guys use fiberglass composite rods with crankbaits," he notes. "The theory is that fiberglass has a slower recovery, and it allows a bass to get more of the bait before you bury the hooks.

"But I disagree with this. A bass inhales a bait in the blink of an eye. I don't think it's possible to feel a bite and react so fast that you pull the bait away from the fish. So as far as I'm concerned, the old 'fiberglass is better' theory doesn't hold water.

"So, I use a 7-foot, 100 percent graphite rod (medium-light action) with diving crankbaits. With this rod, I don't feel like I lose anything to fiberglass, plus it has a lot better sensitivity. Crankbait bites can be very subtle, and I believe I can feel some bites on a graphite rod that I can't with a glass rod. With the graphite, I pull the bait down and stop it, and I can feel that little tick."

Cook normally spools his crankbait reel with 10- or 12-pound-test line. He recommends Berkley UltraThin, since its thin diameter yields longer casts and better bait action than standard diameter lines in equivalent weights.

crankbait is that it catches on the limb, and as you stretch your line, it pops off. Lures like the Cordell Big O and Norman Big N are what I call intense deflection baits because they ricochet off objects better. Those sudden movements can trigger impulsive strikes from moody bass."

The drawback, he adds, is that lures with squared-off bills tend to hang up easier and won't dive as deep as round-bill lures.

When fish are aggressive, the amount of wiggle in a crankbait is not as critical as it is when they're fussy. As a rule, wide-wobbling crankbaits that displace a lot of water and emit strong vibrations tend to work better in stained or muddy water. However, pros' opinions vary on that subject.

For example, pros like VanDam and Mark Davis prefer tight-wiggling lures (like the Shad Rap, Deep Little N, Model 6A Bomber and Fat Free Shad) when fishing cold water. They say the tighter wiggle allows the bait to be worked at slower speeds.

"The key to cold water is to slow down the retrieve," confirms Davis. "A tight-wiggling bait still produces good action on the slow retrieve."

VanDam points to the Shad Rap as an example of a tight-wiggling bait that is popular for fishing clear, cold water during the early spring.

"It's got an extremely tight wiggle and no rattles," he explains. "There's a case where the subtlety of the bait is its strong suit because there are times when big, noisy lures can spook fish, such as the early pre-spawn season."

And what about lipless crankbaits? Mark Davis says the Cordell Spot is thicker across the back, so it has a wider wobble than the thinner-bodied Rat-L-Trap.

"Either brand works well when you're fishing them near the surface," he explains. "But I prefer thicker lipless baits for fishing deeper water, because the thicker body has more water resistance and will vibrate more at slower speeds."

NOISEMAKERS

The pros agree that the amount of water a crankbait moves as it's pulled through the water plays a role in a lure's success. As a crankbait wiggles throughout the retrieve, it displaces water that is converted to vibrations, which bass sense through their lateral lines. All crankbaits displace water, but when visibility is limited, such as in muddy water, lures that emit more vibration tend to be more effective.

Contrary to common belief, flat-sided crankbaits displace more water than round-bodied crankbaits and tend to have tighter wiggles.

"A round crankbait is more aqua-dynamic in that water slides over and around it,

Getting a bass to bite a crankbait is one matter; boating it is another. Ken Cook says many anglers fail to fight fish properly. They simply hold on and reel, and this opens the door for escape.

"The problem comes when a bass jumps," Cook explains. "Many crankbaits are compact and heavy, and they're easy to throw. So you want to keep that fish down in the water and tire it out before landing it."

When a bass latches on to his crankbait, Cook reels it to within 20 feet of the boat, then he stops reeling and allows the fish to struggle against the line and rod. "I turn my electric motor at an angle where the boat will go in a circle, and I start dragging the fish round and round. Meanwhile, I stick my rod as far into the water as I can get it to pull down on the fish when it tries to jump. Then I just hold on until the fish wears itself out. When I've won the fight, I reel it in and lip it."

Cook emphasizes that anglers lose bass on crankbaits because they "get the fish too close to the boat too fast. They're still hot, and they get away. But by fighting fish out away from the boat, there's more room for error. So be patient, and also be sure your hooks are needle sharp."

so it doesn't move as much water," explains Clunn. "But that changes as the body size increases. A large, rounded crankbait displaces more water than a smaller, rounded crankbait."

VanDam says rattles help compensate for the lack of water displacement in round-bodied crankbaits, but noise is less of a concern in flat-sided lures because of the enhanced vibration.

WIND AND UNCLEAR water are two conditions that influence crankbait fishing success.

"I consider the flat-sided crankbaits a more natural presentation because the vibrations are there, yet they're more subtle," he explains. "If I've got two lures with similar characteristics in depth and action, I prefer the flat one over a round one."

Noise is another consideration and probably a factor we know least about, insists Clunn, who has tested crankbait sounds with an underwater listening device. Although lures with rattles have proved to be effective, little is known about which types of sounds fool fish in different situations.

"Crankbaits probably are the noisiest baits we fish, including those without rattles," he says. "The lure harnesses and split rings clatter as the lure wiggles, so that may have bearing as well."

Most pros agree that rattling lures work well in dingy, warm water or around heavy cover, whereas less noise is preferred in clear, calm water.

Trying to apply all of the variables to your fishing may be mind-boggling at first, but once you learn to recognize the subtle differences, the crankbait puzzle will become easier to solve.

GUIDE TO CRANKBAITS AND JERKBAITS

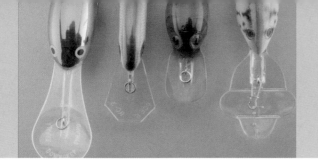

A CRANKBAIT'S bill is the contact point for deflecting off cover. Experiment with different shapes to find what action attracts the most strikes.

CRANKBAIT PICKS OF THE PROS

Crankbait experts discuss
their favorite crankbaits and the situations
in which they are most effective

THERE'S NOTHING WRONG with letting confidence guide you through the crankbait selection process — provided your confidence lies in more than one or two lures.

Pro anglers also have favorite models, but their level of confidence runs deeper into the tacklebox. Through hours of on-the-water experience and testing, they develop a systematic approach to crankbait tactics that calls upon specific lures for specific tasks.

(Opposite page) MIKE AUTEN likes crankbaits with squared bills that careen off solid objects.

"Anyone who thinks all crankbaits that appear similar perform the same way is missing out on some of the keys to crankbait fishing success," explains Kevin VanDam.

VanDam says each model within most brands has inherent characteristics that give that bait certain performance traits. The subtle differences may be in how the bait floats or suspends, wiggles, deflects off objects or emits vibrations as it moves through the water — any one of which can trigger a bass to strike under the right conditions.

Therefore, when pro crankers select lures for given situations, they analyze the conditions and then match the lures that will provide optimum performance within those conditions. Read on to learn about the crankbaits used by the tour's lipped lure gurus.

Crankbait Tips

Crankbaits are ideal tournament lures. During practice, they can be used to comb large areas quickly to "bird-dog" active fish — it would take much longer to cover the same amount of water with a worm or jig. They are also perfect when probing offshore structure, such as humps, points, stumprows and dropoffs in the 12- to 20-foot zone, where bass often congregate in warm weather.

Cranking Reels

Most effective cranking can be facilitated by varying the retrieve speed of the reel used. For most situations, a 5:1 reel is ideal. A slow retrieve (3:1) reel is good for early spring or late fall, when the water is cool and the bass are sluggish. It also makes all-day fishing with the larger deep divers less fatiguing. High speed (6:1) reels are useful in warm water. They let the angler "burn" a crankbait for active fish while turning the reel at a normal rate of speed.

SHALLOW RUNNERS
(1 To 6 Feet)

• **_Bagley BB3 and B Flat/Mike Auten_** — "Both lures run about 3 feet deep and are good alternatives for the types of areas where other anglers may prefer a spinnerbait. The squared lip on the BB3 deflects well off hard objects and the big body and wide wobble displaces a lot of water, so I like it for cranking around laydowns and boat docks during the fall. The B Flat has a wider wobble and displaces more water. The highly buoyant baits are more snagless than most crankbaits."

• **_Bagley Kill'r B2/Shaw Grigsby_** — "I like to work the Kill'r B2 through limbs and lily pads with a slow retrieve. The lip causes the bait to kick away from cover, which triggers strikes in summer or fall when fish corral shad against bushy banks."

• **_Bomber Flat A/Mark Davis_** — "The bait has a tight wiggle and near-neutral buoyancy, making it my choice for cold, shallow water. You can slow it down without sacrificing the action or depth, which is important when bass are sluggish. The slow rising characteristic makes it good for fishing over grass in cold water, because you can use a stop-and-go retrieve yet keep the bait in the strike zone."

• **_Cordell Big O/Denny Brauer_** — "I go to this when following other anglers who are fishing spinnerbaits and jigs around wood in 3 feet of water or less, or when fishing rocky banks during the spring. Because of its small size, the C77 model appeals to numbers of fish, but I will use larger sizes if bigger fish are in the area. The lure has a wide wobble, runs true and casts extremely well with heavy line and baitcast gear."

• **_Mann's 1-Minus/Paul Elias_** — "This is my choice when I can't fish a lipless crankbait through thick, submerged grass or brush, or in river backwater areas where other anglers are using worms and spinnerbaits. I fish it on a high speed reel and 17-pound line."

• **_Norman Baby N/Rob Kilby_** — "Given its 2-inch size and short bill, the lure is ideal when shad are small and holding around wood in the backs of creeks during the summer and fall. I use 17-pound test and throw it into the same places where other anglers are using spinnerbaits."

• **_Storm Pro Short Wart/Ken Cook_** — "The small size and heavy vibration make it ideal for murky, shallow water and in brush when small baitfish are present, such as during the fall when other anglers are fishing spinnerbaits around stumps in creeks."

MIDDEPTH RUNNERS (6 To 10 Feet)

• **_Bomber Model 6A, 7A/Kevin VanDam_** — "I prefer the 6A for cold water because it has a smaller profile and a slightly tighter wiggle, which I like in water below 60 degrees. It comes through rocks and trees well and rights itself quickly when bouncing off objects. The 7A has similar weedless characteristics, but its slightly wider wobble makes it more effective in warmer water. The lip on the 7A angles downward slightly, so it runs shallower than the smaller 6A model. With 10-pound test and a long cast, I can get the 7A to 8 or 9 feet; the 6A reaches 10 feet. Don't exceed 17-pound-test line with the 6A or you lose action; the 7A maintains its wobble integrity with 20-pound test or less."

• **_Mann's Paul's Crankbait/Paul Elias_** — "My first choice for fishing river ledges in 7 to 10 feet of water because it has nearly the same buoyancy as wooden lures, which helps it back out of snags and grass. It also casts into the wind easily, which affords longer casts to get the bait deeper. It will run 12 feet on 10-pound line, but I prefer to use 12 pound. You can create a wide wobble by slowing the retrieve, or change to a tighter wiggle by increasing retrieve speed."

• **_Norman Deep Little N/O.T. Fears_** — "It has a fairly tight wiggle and runs 8 to 10 feet deep, making it a good coldwater bait. One of the keys when I won the Lanier tournament last December was that I cranked it slowly, then hesitated when the lure bumped into a rock, log or dock piling."

• *Rebel Deep Wee R/Mark Davis* — "This small, fairly buoyant bait fishes well around hard cover and is my choice for bouncing over rocks. The unique rattle sound seems to appeal to bass on those days when other crankbaits don't. It has a tight wiggle and is good in clear water. It runs 6 feet deep on 10-pound test and is best-suited for 8- to 12-pound-test line."

• *Storm Wiggle Wart/Ken Cook* — "The wide wobble and big body make this one good in spring when fishing cold, muddy water. It maintains its vibrations on a slow retrieve and runs about 8 feet (on 10-pound line)."

DEEP RUNNERS (10 To 20 Feet)

• *Bagley DB3/Shaw Grigsby* — "Because of its wide wobble and buoyancy, it has good deflection qualities and will "back up" from solid snags if you slow or stop the retrieve when you hit something. I use it for fishing creek ledges and dropoffs. It runs about 12 feet on 12-pound test."

• *Bomber Fat Free Shad/Mark Davis* — "The bait that helped me win the 1995 Bassmaster Classic has some design principles that set it apart from others. Compared to most big bodied baits, this one has a relatively tight wiggle, which makes it a good choice for slow cranking in cold water. The body is less rounded than most deep crankbaits so it displaces a lot of water to help bass find it in stained water, and it doesn't lose its wiggle when deflecting through cover. It runs about 17 feet on 10-pound test, but I prefer to throw it on heavier line. It works well on 25-pound test for banging across shallower bottoms, too. However, it's a quality-fish bait, so if you're around little fish, it shouldn't be your first choice."

• *Mann's 20-Plus and 30-Plus/Paul Elias* — "A good choice when deep water bass want a big bait digging on bottom, especially along deep ledges. Some baits momentarily lose their action when they bounce along bottom, but this one stays in the search mode when it bounces off objects. It has a wide wobble, and the big bill rides over limbs and protects the hooks. The 20-Plus runs about 15 feet on 12-pound line, while the 30 will touch 22 feet on 17-pound line."

• *Norman DD22/O.T. Fears* — "The moderate-action wiggle makes it a good spring/summer bait for reaching 15-foot depths. It casts into the wind easily, so it's well-suited for long casts over deep, main lake bars."

• *Storm Magnum Wiggle Wart/David Ashcraft* — "The big bodied, large billed bait will run 12 feet on 12-pound line. The slightly upturned bill makes it effective for fishing shallow rock jetties because the lure retains its action while banging along bottom. If necessary, I use 20-pound-test line to slow the nose wiggle and make the tail more erratic."

DAVID FRITTS says deep bass usually aren't as aggressive, so he chooses a crankbait with a tight action that resembles the swimming action of a baitfish.

PICKING THE RIGHT CRANKBAIT

A Complete Rundown
On Choosing And Using Metal,
Wood And Plastic Crankbaits ...

RICK CLUNN BELIEVES unique flat crankbaits without rattles produce a sound perceived by bass to be a crippled baitfish.

SLIM DOWN ON CRANKBAITS

Rick Clunn won't leave an area where he's been catching bass without trying a flat-sided diving plug

THROUGHOUT THE AGES, mankind has been infatuated with spherical objects. Christopher Columbus sailed into the unknown to prove the world was round. Ancient cultures have worshipped the sun. Men have dreamed of flying to the moon for thousands of years, and finally reached the orb in 1969.

Even bass anglers have their own spherical fixation when selecting crankbaits. Columbus had a difficult time convincing the Spanish royalty to fund his expedition, and today's lure sellers have just about as much trouble persuading Bassmasters to buy flat-sided crankbaits. Whether for deep cranking or burning the shallows, the round, wide wobbling crankbait has become the most popular choice for many applications.

Flat, lipless crankbaits have always been fan favorites, but stick a bill on it, and bass anglers treat this flat lure like an ugly duckling. However, pros on the Bassmaster Tour know these slim plugs catch bass when the fat ones fail.

Skinny crankbaits are proven fish catchers, as pointed out by these experts on the flat-sided lures.

GOING FLAT IN SPRING

Virginia pro Curt Lytle prefers throwing flat-sided crankbaits when the water temperature is below 60 degrees. "They're really outstanding early and late in the year," says Lytle. "Most of your flat baits are fairly close to being neutral buoyancy, so they don't pop up."

Early in the year, Lytle selects flat-sides in red or brown hues to imitate crawfish. The lures' neutral buoyancy becomes a key factor during this time, because Lytle wants his lure to stay close to the bottom and mimic a fleeing crawfish. He achieves this presentation with a "real grinding retrieve" that constantly bangs the lure's bill into the clay or rocky floor.

Shad pattern flat-sides (pearl, Tennessee shad or chrome) produce best for Lytle in the fall. Since bass seem to suspend more during this time, Lytle runs his shad imitators at a steady pace. He occasionally tries to bump the lure into something, but most of the time, he keeps it running in the middepth zone.

Slick clay and tapering gravel banks are two of Lytle's favorite areas to throw flat crankbaits. "A lot of times, the flat crankbait will work where other people don't fish," he suggests. "For that reason, you can catch fish on a flat crankbait with almost no cover around you." If the clean banks in a cove all look the same, Lytle recommends targeting the windblown shores first.

Lytle prefers skinny crankbaits for shallow water situations. "There are very few flat-sides that will work past 8 feet," he warns. Most of his slim plugs run between 3 and 7 feet deep.

He relies on three models of flat-sides for various applications. Although he rarely fishes these lures in heavy cover, Lytle occasionally runs a Poe's RC3 through objects, because he believes it deflects better than other flat-sides. He opts for a prototype Hawg Caller crankbait for running in medium cover and prefers the thin-sided Rapala Shad Rap for fishing along open banks. "It doesn't deflect well off cover, but it does trigger strikes in open water," claims Lytle.

Crankbait Tips

Storm Manufacturing's ThinFin was the first flat-sided crankbait to gain a national following. Introduced in 1965, this lure was conceived as a visual simulation of a threadfin shad. Designed as a floater/diver, the lure proved to be an overnight success, selling a million units in its first 18 months on the market.

Flat Good Bait

A lure designer of flat-sided crankbaits should know its intricacies and so should you.

"Being thinner, a flat crankbait has less buoyancy than a fat one," says designer Jim Gowing. "If you stop a fat crankbait during the retrieve, it will float up quickly. But a thin one will rise much more slowly, thanks to its slender design.

"This can be both a plus and a minus. To me, its reduced buoyancy makes a flat crankbait more visually appealing to the bass, because a live minnow doesn't float to the surface when it stops moving. But many anglers are used to their crankbaits floating up when they're fishing heavy cover with them. These fishermen may hang up a thin crankbait more until they get used to its different characteristics."

Gowing fishes a flat-sided lure like the Flat A "more like a spinnerbait than a fat crankbait." The lure designer recommends that when casting these baits around brush and stumps, a slow, deliberate retrieve be employed.

"Just slow crank the bait," he coaches. "Don't let up on the retrieve when you feel the lure contact cover — just keep on reeling. Stopping the bait will expose the hooks to the cover and result in more hang-ups. Simply winding down on the lure will cause it to roll right over the obstacle. The stop-and-go retrieve so often favored by anglers with fat, deep diving crankbaits isn't the best way to go with these lures."

Whenever possible, Lytle tries to match his crankbait with baitfish size, but most of the time he throws larger flat-sides because the lures are easier to cast. He uses spinning tackle for the lightweight No. 7 Shad Rap, but selects baitcasting gear (7-foot medium action rod and Shimano Castaic reel) for the rest of his flat plugs. In most situations, Lytle opts for 10-pound-test line. When casting into the wind, however, he pares down to 8-pound test for his spinning gear.

While tinkering with these lures, Lytle has discovered that flat-sides work best when left alone. He has tweaked the bills, but his modifications caused the lures to run awry. "Most of them are made of wood, and a lot of wood crankbaits have their own personality anyway, so you tend not to modify them much," he says.

FLAT CRANKBAITS typically run shallow, making them effective tools for finding prespawn fish staging near spawning areas.

CLEAR CHOICE

Kentucky pro Terry Bolton relies on a Bomber Flat A crankbait in the spring, when the water temperature remains in the 40s to mid-50s. He prefers the tight wiggle of the Flat A in clear water over the wide wobble of his other springtime favorite, the round-shaped Rebel Wee R. "It seems like the Flat A is a little better in cleaner water," he claims.

Baitfish are the main forage of bass in the colder water, so Bolton opts for a crankbait that best resembles the prey. "The profile of a Flat A seems to imitate a shad or a bluegill, while the Wee R is better at imitating a crawfish," suggests Bolton. He selects flat crankbaits in shad hues for clear water situations; and chartreuse/black, chartreuse/brown or firetiger for stained water.

THE NARROW BODY of a flat crankbait prevents it from floating up quickly. As a result, the bait remains at a constant depth on a steady retrieve.

Flat-sides produce best for Bolton along prespawn staging areas in creeks or at the mouths of bays. His favorite targets for cranking include 45 degree banks and points or flats close to channel swings. He also likes to run the Flat A through the tops of hydrilla beds. "The lure's tight wiggle sheds the grass very well," says Bolton.

The Flat A allows Bolton to cover depths ranging from 2 to 9 feet, depending on the line size he selects. When fishing around cover, Bolton chooses 12-pound test, but scales down to 8- to 10-pound test to give the lure better action and make it run deeper along open banks. He attests the lure runs its maximum depth of 9 feet when tied on 8-pound line.

Bolton cranks the Flat A to the bottom and then employs a slow, steady retrieve. "The Flat A is a little narrower body, so it doesn't float up as quickly," he advises. "So once you get the bait down, it does a real good job of staying down."

The Kentucky angler usually cranks the lure at a steady pace, but occasionally varies his retrieve with a stop-and-go presentation. Even though he tries to cover a lot of water during the spring, Bolton favors a slower retrieve that prevents him from fishing too fast, which he has a tendency to do, especially after catching a bass.

LIGHT LINE fished on spinning gear enables flat crankbaits to run deeper and impart a more realistic action.

While testing crankbaits in a swimming pool, Bolton noticed the Flat A has a different deflection angle than round models. "Whenever you hit a rock or something with that flat bait, it has a very erratic action — more erratic than a Wee R or Bomber Model A," he says. Bolton adds that the Flat A deflects as much as 2 to 3 feet away from an object, whereas a round crankbait usually slides along the object it hits.

A 7-foot G. Loomis cranking rod with a Shimano baitcast reel (5.1:1 gear ratio) works best for most of Bolton's flat-side cranking tactics. However, he

WHEN USING flat crankbaits in cold water, Clunn makes the lure dive by sweeping the rod. Then, he pauses it briefly before making the next sweep.

does switch to a 6-foot medium-light Loomis spinning rod and a Shimano spinning reel with 8-pound-test line for making long casts to get his lure deeper, or for fishing on blustery days. He notes the Flat A is difficult to throw, since it catches wind and sails like "a butterfly with hiccups."

CHANGE-UP BAIT

Rick Clunn believes the bass' lateral line is a sophisticated screening device. "They can differentiate slight details and differences in lures through a hydrodynamic imaging process that we can't even comprehend," he says. "What this really tells you is that no bait is necessarily any better than another all the time, but sometimes, using different baits is really the key."

The flat crankbait shines as a change-up lure for Clunn when he fishes reservoirs with grassbeds, such as Sam Rayburn or Seminole. He opts for a subtle presentation when anglers throwing Rat-L-Traps have pounded these lakes for several weeks. "I go right behind guys who have beaten the water to death, and catch fish on that quieter bait," says Clunn. "It's not nearly as obtrusive to the fish as those baits that have all the rattles."

Retrieving his skinny crankbaits at a medium to fast clip produces best for Clunn. "Every bait has a signature vibration when you reel it, and you can feel it all the way through the line to the rod tip," advises Clunn. "A medium to high speed

CLUNN BELIEVES a flat crankbait produces more vibrations in a shorter distance.

FLAT CRANKBAITS can be a productive alternative to lip-less crankbaits.

creates that signature in the flat bait that I know generates the majority of the bites."

The flat-side also serves as an alternate lure for a cold weather presentation. While others sweep a suspending Rebel Spoonbill Minnow, Clunn prefers a flat-side, because it casts into the wind better than jerkbaits. The crankbait specialist makes the lure dive by sweeping his rod. Then, he pauses it for a three-count before making the next sweep.

Whether sweeping or burning the crankbait, Clunn works the lure with his signature series Bass Pro Shops heavy action 7-foot rod and a high speed Bass Pro Shops (6.3:1 gear ratio) baitcast reel. When fishing shallow weeds, Clunn ties his lures on 14- to 17-pound-test line, but switches to 12-pound fluorocarbon for sweeping the crankbait in cold, clear water.

Replacing the factory hooks with the next-largest-size trebles is the only modification Clunn makes to his flat-sided crankbait. "It's just a good all-around bait," praises Clunn. "It's one I always have tied on, and I won't leave fish without throwing it. That bait has shown me over and over that it will generate strikes when fish quit hitting anything else."

Slimming Down

Jim Gowing designed Bomber's Flat A, a companion lure to the popular fat-bodied Model A and long, rounded Long A. But he believes there is a time and a place to fish flat-sided cranks, just as there is for the other designs.

"Flat crankbaits are especially productive in cold water, prespawn conditions," he believes. "They're dynamite on staging bass, fish that have moved up out of deep water and are holding in certain areas prior to moving even shallower to spawn. Most pros use them in the initial tournaments of the year, before the bass go on the bed."

The reason these lures work so well in cold water, Gowing reasons, is their tighter vibration. "You'd expect to find less active baitfish in cold water, and this is exactly what the tight wiggle of a flat crankbait simulates," he says. "It's far more realistic under these conditions than the slow, wide wobble of a fat lure."

When retrieved, a flat crank repeatedly tilts right and left, producing a fluttering action that's more like that of a thin metal lure like a Gay Blade than a potbellied crankbait.

"By contrast, a fat crank pivots in an X pattern, producing a wide, thumping wobble," he says. "Bass relate much better to this more pronounced action when the water temperature is over 60 degrees."

A flat crankbait produces "more action in a shorter distance," Gowing adds. "Let's say you measured a distance of 10 feet, through which you retrieved both a thin and a flat crankbait. The flat one will produce more wiggles over the same distance, but they'll be tighter than those produced by the fat lure. The flat crank will also throw more flash, since the flat sides gather and reflect more light than rounded sides. Underwater, a flat crankbait with a reflective finish looks like a strobe light."

Gowing also prefers a flat crankbait in current. "There's less drag on the lure than you'd get from a fatter design," he explains. "If you were fishing around a rock jetty in a tailwater, for example, you'd find that a fat crankbait would tend to get swept away in the current and may miss its mark when you retrieved it. A flat one, on the other hand, would knife through the current. Many tailwater fishermen cast a flat crankbait downstream and simply tight-line it in heavy current. This technique will catch bass, white bass, stripers, hybrids and trout."

USE SMALL crankbaits when fishing shallow water that has been hit hard by other anglers.

CRANKBAIT FINESSE

On a slow day, tiny diving plugs will add pounds to your catch and a broad smile to your face

I F YOU STOCK YOUR TACKLEBOX with only those lures that win bass tournaments, you may be omitting some valuable fish catchers that can save the day when all else fails.

No one will argue that the power tactics — big spinnerbaits, crankbaits and jigs fished on heavy tackle and line — dominate tourney wins. But don't think for a minute that a pro's bag of tricks doesn't include presentations at the opposite end of the spectrum.

Ron Shuffield is a prime example. The rugged Arkansan is well-known for wrestling big bass out of thick cover with a jig, 20-pound-plus line and a stout flippin' rod. The record will show that his major wins and high finishes were the direct result of strong-arm tactics.

What the record doesn't show, however, is that there are times when his tools are small crankbaits — usually Rapala Shad Raps — dainty line and light spinning tackle.

"There are special situations and conditions when bass aren't going to run down bigger baits or are keying on small baitfish. At those times, they often require a more subtle presentation," he explains. "Finesse crankbaiting — which is what I call it — will not only save the day, but produce a good limit in a hurry."

Missouri pro Randy Blaukat mentions other reasons finesse cranking has become another tool in the pros' arsenals. Like Shuffield, Blaukat is better known for power tactics, yet he's a firm believer in the puny presentation.

"Keep in mind that it's not a primary

(Opposite page) **IN SUMMERTIME, when burning spinnerbaits around logs and across flats is trendy, savvy anglers use small crankbaits to trick jaded fish.**

Crankbait Tip

When a bass strikes a crankbait, it may be only lightly hooked. A hard, sudden hook set — the kind used with a plastic worm or jig — may rip the hook out of the fish. Instead, with the rod tip low, sweep the rod to the side really quickly. The super-sharp hooks used by most crankbait manufacturers will sink deeper as the fish struggles.

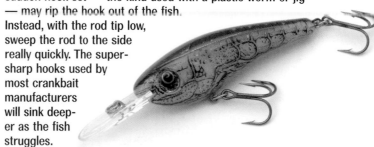

Etiquette For Cranking Finesse

Finesse crankbaiting isn't without its challenges. Finesse-style plugs have small treble hooks that make it difficult to keep a fish hooked, and fishing them on light tackle can provide some anxious moments.

Replacing little trebles with the next-size-larger may work, but be careful that doing so doesn't kill the action. Hoosier Mark Randolph says that the additional weight of some hooks will alter the lure's wobble, and bigger hooks can tangle under the lure's belly.

"I have discovered that Eagle Claw's Featherlites allow me to upsize hooks on some baits without hurting the action," he says. "But you still may have to deal with the tangling problem."

Another solution, he adds, is to put two split rings on the tail-hook hanger before adding a hook. The double split rings will allow the hook to swivel more, which makes it less likely to pry loose from the fish's mouth.

"That works best with a Shad Rap because it's a longer bait," he notes. "It's a neat trick when the bass are only taking the bait from the rear. On the downside, it can cause more tangling with the belly hook. Sometimes I'll remove the front treble and hope the rear hook does the job."

Here are more tips to improve your efficiency:

• Tie direct to tiny lures — Snaps are OK for larger lures, but finesse crankbaits will work better when the line is connected directly to a split ring.

• Change line often — A day of cranking with a spinning outfit puts strain on light line and will cause it to twist more.

• Don't wind against the drag — That puts twist in the line and guarantees a snarled mess on subsequent casts.

• Close the bail by hand — Turning the reel handle to snap it shut can put loops in the spooled line. After the cast, fold the bail and lift with the rod tip to remove slack from the line, and you'll reduce problems.

• Spray spool with silicone — Use 100 percent pure Silicone or Blakemore's Line Magic. It relaxes the line and adds casting distance.

DOWNSIZING TO small crankbaits can up the ante on strikes when the larger models fail to produce.

method for tournament anglers, because we're fishing for the heaviest stringer, and the power presentations are going to produce bigger bass," he explains. "But several of us do rely upon smaller baits to catch a limit before targeting the big sacks that people read about."

Well, like the experts say, read on.

FINESSE IS IN

Recreational anglers should take a closer look at finesse cranking, Blaukat adds.

"These types of baits are outstanding for the angler who simply wants to catch fish, because little crankbaits produce more strikes from a variety of fish than the bigger, more publicized versions," he explains. "And on really tough days, it may be the only crankbait that is going to get you strikes."

What constitutes a finesse crankbait often is in the eyes of a beholder. As a rule, it's a small-bodied, shallow diving lure that weighs less than 1/4 ounce,

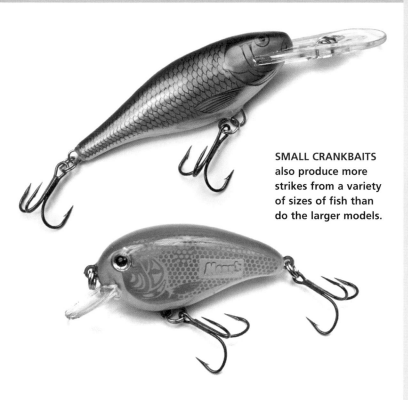

SMALL CRANKBAITS also produce more strikes from a variety of sizes of fish than do the larger models.

Tackling For Finesse

Randy Blaukat likes to pitch tiny crankbaits around cover with a 7-foot spinning outfit spooled with 6- to 10-pound line. The spinning outfit is a lot more efficient at putting small baits in the strike zone, he says.

"I've gotten comfortable fishing light line around cover, and you've got to use light line to cast those little baits," he explains. "I like to fish them on a stop-and-go retrieve, and I'll twitch them intermittently."

Line size is critical to the action of some lures and dictates how far you can cast them. As a rule, 6- to 10-pound monofilament works best on spinning, and the smaller line enables lures to run deeper and vibrate more effectively.

"Large-spool reels enhance casting distance and reduce the problems of line snarls on spinning reels," notes Ron Shuffield, who fishes his Shad Raps on 8-pound P-Line and a 7-foot Pinnacle rod and DeadBolt spinning reel.

Most finesse crankers use medium action spinning rods in lengths from 6 to 7 feet. The 7-foot rod enables longer casts and provides more leverage when playing fish, but shorter rods are more efficient when fishing around docks or timber.

Mark Randolph has found Berkley's Center Drag reels, Fenwick Techna AV spinning rods and 10-pound Berkley Big Game line to be his best combination. Blaukat fishes the Marukin on a 6-6 MegaBass spinning outfit and 6-pound Nitlon monofilament.

Playing big fish snagged on crankbaits with small hooks and on rods spooled with light line gets tricky. Horsing a quality fish can produce heartbreaking results.

"The first thing to remember is that you don't have to use a heavy hook set — most of the time, the fish hook themselves," says Randolph. "Second, if you trust the drag, use it. Frankly, I prefer to back-reel, because I can control fish better that way."

Back-reeling is a simple matter of disengaging the reel's anti-reverse and allowing the fish to take line. The angler controls the reverse-rotating reel handle so he can resume cranking instantly.

"Yes, you're going to lose some fish because of the small baits and light line," says Randolph. "But remember: You got those strikes because of the finesse lure and tackle. When fishing is tough, isn't it best to take those kinds of chances?"

works best on small diameter line and is too light to throw on heavy baitcast gear.

Unless, of course, you're Rick Clunn. The four time Bassmaster Classic champion once revealed that his secret lure on heavily pressured lakes is a crappie pattern Norman Tiny N, a 1/8-ounce diver that runs less than 4 feet deep.

However, he uses it with the same Bass Pro Shops' 7-foot baitcast outfit and 15-pound line that he uses for traditional crankbaiting, explaining that he believes he is more efficient with baitcast tackle despite the restriction in casting distance.

"I'm not very good with spinning tackle, and I don't like changing tackle during a day of fishing," he describes. "It may work well for others, but this works best for me."

Having said that, Clunn agrees that tiny crankbaits are ideal for

recreational fishermen because they catch so many fish, and they may be easier for others to use on spinning tackle.

"Finesse crankbaits are so good, in fact, that they can become a detriment to the tournament angler who gets caught up in hooking small fish," he explains. "A tournament fisherman has to discipline himself to sacrifice bites to win a tournament. A recreational angler doesn't have to deal with that element and can have a great day with a small crankbait tied to his line."

PROVEN TRACK RECORD

None of this is new to Mark Randolph, a Monticello, Ind., angler skilled in finessing with cranks. Randolph, who grew up fishing for stream bass with light tackle and small crankbaits, considers finesse cranking his primary pattern in major bass tournaments.

"First, it's a pattern most anglers ignore," Randolph explains. "Second, I like to cover a lot of water and target active fish along the banks, so the technique is a natural. I know I'm going to get a lot of bites."

It's perfectly suited for fishing lakes that are getting hammered by other anglers, adds Randolph, and one you can use with confidence when fishing behind other anglers.

"That strategy has won me a lot of money around smaller lakes in Indiana," says Randolph. "Eighty percent of the fish I catch on these lures come from banks that have been fished by other anglers."

That includes shorelines covered with docks, where he will pitch or skip small crankbaits into the same places others might fish jigs.

"When everyone is fishing docks, you'd be surprised how many bass you can catch behind them by pitching little crankbaits under or alongside the piers," he offers.

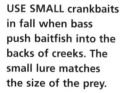

USE SMALL crankbaits in fall when bass push baitfish into the backs of creeks. The small lure matches the size of the prey.

SEASONAL FINESSE

Some seasonal patterns are tailor-made for finesse cranking. Shuffield finds his aforementioned Shad Rap pattern deadly during the prespawn, when bass are beginning to prowl the shallows.

"The No. 5 and No. 7 Shad Raps are the first lures to produce when the fish begin to stage around secondary points in clear water lakes," he says. "The Shad Rap matches the size of forage the fish are targeting, and its tight, subtle wobble — without a rattle — really seems to work best."

Randolph agrees, noting that when water temperatures on Midwestern lakes rise above 47 degrees, Shad Raps provide the kind of action that provokes strikes from seemingly neutral, coldwater bass.

"You've got a similar situation in late fall, when bass school in the backs of creeks, following the balls of shad," adds Shuffield. "Even though the activity may be over the creek channels in deep water, I will throw that little crankbait into pods of bait and

Crankbait Wizard's Modifications

To ensure that a crankbait reaches its maximum depth, David Fritts puts it through a little "fine-tuning."

The process begins with making sure the lure runs straight when retrieved. Since even the smallest variance can rob the bait of depth, he won't tolerate a bait that tracks as little as 2 inches to one side.

Fritts' technique for tuning an errant crankbait differs slightly from that used by most anglers.

"A lot of people just grab the wire on the bill from the top and bend it one way or the other," he explains. "I lay the pliers on the top of the bill, parallel to the bill, and twist it slightly. That keeps the wire good and tight, so that when you tune one, it usually (maintains) that tuning better."

Fritts twists the line tie in the opposite direction from the way the bait has been veering. That is, if the bait is swimming to the right, he twists the line tie to the left.

To get a little extra depth, he also files down the bottom side of the front of a crankbait's plastic lip to sharpen the front and enable the lure to cut through the water with less friction. But be forewarned: the lip will be weakened and more prone to break.

---

catch bass suspended underneath the shad. Again, I'm matching my lure to the size of the baitfish."

Summertime can be equally effective, says Randolph. While most anglers are burning spinnerbaits around logs and stumps on the flats, he's fishing behind them with little crankbaits, retrieving the bait fast and making it bang bottom and deflect off cover.

"That's when I go to the Cordell Big O (Model C77), because it has a great wobble, it rattles and it comes through brush extremely well," he explains.

The Big O is Randolph's bread-and-butter finesse crankbait, one he says has produced in just about every lake he has fished. The C77 Model weighs 1/3 ounce and runs 4 to 5 feet deep on 10-pound line. Color choices depend upon what the fish are targeting, but the Super Shad, Crawdad and Fire Tiger are his mainstays.

"During the dog days of August, I find the smallest 'Fat A' (1/16 ounce) is better," says Randolph. "I don't know why, but fish seem to eat it better in hot weather."

Blaukat also drops to smaller sizes during postspawn and late summer, opting for the diminutive MegaBass' Marukin or Griffon crankbaits. The 1/8-ounce Marukin is only about 1 inch long — hence, it resembles fry that have abandoned nesting areas.

"It's really effective on northern river systems, where fishing can get tough and the bass tend to run smaller," he explains. "It's got a fairly wide wobble, runs about 2 feet deep and can produce a limit quickly when bass are holding around shallow water cover. It's also good when the water gets hot in late summer."

A SMALL CRANKBAIT finessed across cover is more effective than a bigger lure on highly pressured fisheries.

GOING ULTRALIGHT WITH CRANKS

For more bass per cast, try these tricks for fishing tiny diving baits

SOME SAY IT'S THE ULTIMATE form of angling for bass. It's ultralight cranking, and it's fishing's version of wingshooting with a .410 — except much more productive.

Casting and retrieving these little diving baits effectively is a specialized art, one that produces consistently — year-round in many regions — and, at times, can outperform any other lure known to man.

Arkansas pro angler Jim Nolan and lure designers like Lee Sisson, along with fishing guides like Jerry Simpson of Missouri — each admits that he was originally attracted to ultralight crankbaiting because of the sheer enjoyment involved.

They have found it to be pleasure fishing in its purest form — but not a pursuit for the faint-hearted.

"I've caught a lot of fish every way you can catch fish, but when I get out on a lake or a little pond by myself, I just take my ultralight outfit and crankbaits smaller than most people have ever seen," says Sisson, who has an 8-pound bass on 2-pound-test line to his credit. "No thrill can rival the one I get when hooking into a fish of any size on these little crankbaits, watching that rod bend and feeling the fish take line."

"Whenever I can get my customers to take the time to learn to fish these little baits, they usually fall in love with this kind of fishing," says Simpson, a guide on Lake of the Ozarks. "Not

Crankbait Tip
Use a 1/4-ounce crankbait with a diving lip when fishing shallow mud or gravel flats in early spring. Root the lure slowly along the bottom so it kicks up silt just like a live crawfish. Red, firetiger or crawfish colors often work best with this presentation.

only do these little lures produce bass, but they'll catch so many other species, like bream, that it keeps my guide parties in action all the time."

GEARING DOWN FOR TINY CRANKS

To understand the passion of these anglers toward ultralight crankbait fishing, it's important to realize just what the sport involves. The equipment usually consists of ultralight spinning gear (although a few companies, like Quantum with its 1510 reel, make baitcasting tackle that will suf-fice). Basic needs are a rod limber enough to cast 1/8-ounce or smaller plugs, but with the right amount of backbone to apply some pressure to the fish without breaking the line, and a small reel with a reliable drag and other machinery.

Ultralight crankbaiting involves lines from 2- to 6-pound test, hardly the stuff of tournament champions.

And then there are the tiny crankbaits, which generally run 3 to 10 feet deep. Most are less than 2 inches long and weigh less than 1/4 ounce. They

The Quirks of Ultralight Cranks

The foremost drawback with ultralight crankbaits is a significant loss of depth compared to its larger counterparts. With a smaller lip and diving plane (the top and back surfaces of the lure, which help drive the bait deeper), the tiny crankbaits won't usually penetrate the 10-foot level. That is true despite the fact that the small diameter line presents very little resistance moving through the water.

But Lee Sisson and Jerry Simpson have come up with a couple of ways of doctoring the small lures to attain more depth. Sisson often attaches a small bell-sinker to the 0-ring of the belly hook of his crankbait, while Simpson has had good success using a large slip sinker attached above a swivel a foot or more from his lure.

"This is almost like a Carolina worm rig," says Simpson, whose favorite ultralight crankbait is Rebel's Teeny Wee Crawfish, a tiny, lifelike lure that has a legion of followers throughout the country. "It will run fine at a fairly great depth, and you can get great action by stopping your retrieve, letting the bait slowly float up and then starting your retrieve again. This makes the lure suspend for a second and then dart toward the bottom."

Another disadvantage is that ultralight crankbaits can't very well penetrate grassbeds or swim through thick treetops. The lures are not weedless in any sense of the word. Instead, they are limited to open water situations, or, at most, to cranking the edges of weedlines, stickups, rocks and the like.

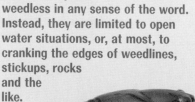

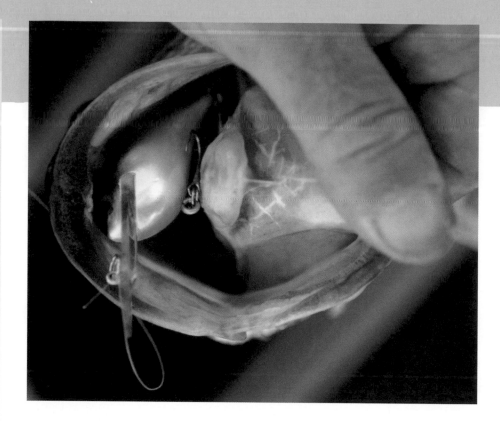

DIMINUTIVE BAITS don't scare away smaller fish as do larger baits. Consequently, they will produce more strikes.

range from minuscule lures like Rebel's Teeny Wee Crawfish (1/10 ounce) to heavier and deeper running lures — like Bagley's Honey B and Lee Sisson Lures' Diving Tiny Ticker.

GOING SMALL MEANS CONSISTENCY

While the sporting nature of such fishing is an attraction to many, these little crankbaits will also produce fish. Without that facet, there would be no self-respecting ultralight crankbait enthusiasts.

The light line is an important reason why these tiny lures produce consistently. The intelligent bass fisherman knows that line invisibility plays a major role in a lure's ability to attract strikes. Too, lures seem to perform better when they're not weighed down by heavy line. Perhaps even more important, with ultralight crankbaits, bait size doesn't discriminate against smaller bass and other species.

"The main reason these crankbaits catch more fish than larger lures is that they don't scare away the smaller fish like larger baits can," says Sisson, who developed the popular Honey B during the decade he served as the lure designer for the Jim Bagley Bait Co. "With large lures, you're going to catch some small fish, but you're also excluding a certain number of little bass; the small lures don't eliminate anything.

"And a lot of it has to do with the feeding habits of bass and the fact that it's just easier for them to mouth or eat a smaller bait. I think there's some validity to the saying that big lures catch big bass, but you can catch big fish with little lures, too. It's like an elephant eating a peanut."

RETYING KNOTS and checking line for nicks is critical when fishing with ultralight crankbaits.

ULTRALIGHT TIMES

Although true ultralight crankbait enthusiasts aren't picky about when they fish these little lures, there are a couple of situations where the baits are the perfect solution to angling problems.

Nolan uses light line and ultralight diving plugs regularly in the clear waters of his home lake — Arkansas' Bull Shoals. "In water that's super-clear, it's to your advantage to go to a small bait on light line," he says. "In very clear water, the fish have a better chance to examine the lure more closely, and a smaller lure fools them easier. Plus, 4- or 6-pound line is not as visible to fish as heavier line.

"Little crankbaits, like the Honey B, which I use a lot, are fast moving lures, so that helps, too."

The others agree that in clear water, a good tactic is to use a small, fast moving lure that gives bass less time to look it over than do baits like a plastic worm or jig.

While there are some definite advantages to using downsized crankbaits, some disadvantages should be addressed, as well. One handicap light-tackle fishing used to present has been eliminated in recent years. There was a time when light tackle meant flimsy tackle. Today, though, rod, reel and line manufacturers have refined their products into high quality, reliable tools.

Rods are more forgiving of the fisherman's mistakes, while the drag systems on reels are smoother and much more reliable than earlier models. And the drag is a very important part of fishing ultralight crankbaits.

Still, with ultralight fishing, it is critical that you concentrate on the most minute details: Knots must be tied properly and line must be checked often for abrasion. Line should be changed regularly. Hooks must be exceedingly sharp. And reels must be cleaned and lubricated periodically.

Ultralight crankbaits are not discriminating. These little diving plugs will attract fish of all sizes, so you've got to be alert and prepared for the tackle-busting bigmouth that's sure to come along sooner or later.

Thinning the Line

Ultralight cranking is one form of fishing that takes practice to perfect because of the ultralight gear and light line it requires. You aren't born with the skill and sensitivity required for successfully fishing ultralight line. But with enough practice, you will understand that even the lightest line — in the right hands — can handle the biggest bass.

"I think fishing 2-, 4- and 6-pound-test line really hones your skills as a fisherman," Lee Sisson says. "It really polishes your techniques, because you have to play the fish carefully.

"That's a major reason fishermen lose fish so often — they don't play the fish. They're using 14- to 20-pound-test line and they've got their drag tightened down. When a fish hits a lure and there's no 'give' in the line or drag, unless the hook gets into a meaty part of the mouth, the hooks pull out. Light line teaches you how to fight a fish on any size line."

"People often are scared to try this little line after fishing so long with bigger line," agrees Jim Nolan. "With 4-pound test, a fisherman will learn to respect the power of a bass. He'll realize that he can't simply horse a fish in, but he's got to play it, or it'll just break off."

Fishermen adept at using light line, he contends, are more likely to land a bigger percentage of the bigger fish they hook than do people who are spoiled by tough, 12-pound-and-heavier line.

THE LARGE bill of a metal crankbait makes it the most weedless bait in the category.

METAL LIPS: NOT JUST FOR COLLECTORS

Don't count out these old-style warriors from the past

Mark Menendez is not a lure collector.

Yet, among the Kentucky pro's most prized possessions are several 300, 400 and 500 Original Bombers, along with some old Heddon Hellbender and Arbogast Mud-Bug crankbaits. None are particularly valuable in the collector's realm, but they mean the world to Menendez.

"They're baits from the forgotten past. But the bass swimming around today weren't around back then, and they'll still bite them. A lot of fish are being caught on them today, although you don't hear much about it."

"I still catch bass on baits like the Mud-Bug and the metal-lipped Hellbender, with the little spinner on the tail," adds veteran pro Gary Klein.

"They're great lures. I grew up throwing those baits, and bass still bite them.

"The reason I still carry them is that all the fishermen today are getting conditioned to throwing the same things, and the fish are conditioned, too. It's the kind of secret that professional anglers guard — old, forgotten lures that still produce well."

"I think technology has kind of passed them by," Texas pro Alton Jones interjects. "They don't have the fancy finishes and color patterns. But they're still fish catchers."

They are our fathers' crankers — diving plugs that predate the Fred Young, shad-shaped crankbait craze — a craze that remains alive and well today. Metal-billed baits, like the 500 series Original Bomber, were introduced in the 1940s, became popular in the '50s, maintained that status through the '70s, and then disappeared from the bass scene in the '80s.

"I love fishing metal-lipped crankbaits, but, unfortunately, the ones I used to use are no longer in production," complains Arkansas guide Mitch Looper, sounding a similar refrain among many fishermen regarding these baits. "I caught my first 5-pound bass on a Hellbender when I was 14 years old. I have caught a lot of big fish on the old Bomber Waterdog, which is no longer being made. And I still have a couple of the original Whopper Stopper models put away for hard times."

OLD STANDBYS

Although there is a newer class of shallower running, smaller metal-lipped baits, three lures still cling to life in the tackleboxes of knowledgeable pros:

• The old wooden 300, 400 or 500 series Original Bombers are prized possessions. The oldest of the metal-billed baits, the Bomber is, well, bomb-shaped, with a V cut into its painted metal bill, which supports a unique line tie. Since being purchased by PRADCO in the 1980s, the Bomber has been made from plastic, which some anglers believe is inferior to the wooden version. It also doesn't have the famous flotation qualities of the wooden Bombers (which are no longer in production).

"I'm probably most fond of the old Bomber 300 Series, known in most circles as the old 'back-up Bomber,'" Menendez interjects. "It's a 2 1/2-inch bait that will actually back up like a crawfish when you're cranking it and stop it. That's an incredible action for a bass to resist."

• Some believe the Arbogast Mud-Bug is a copy

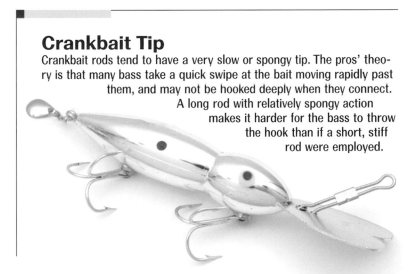

Crankbait Tip
Crankbait rods tend to have a very slow or spongy tip. The pros' theory is that many bass take a quick swipe at the bait moving rapidly past them, and may not be hooked deeply when they connect. A long rod with relatively spongy action makes it harder for the bass to throw the hook than if a short, stiff rod were employed.

Metal Lips For Big Bass

Texas angler Chad Potts scores consistently by fishing a Mud-Bug along shallow banks. "Most of my better big fish days have been on the Mud-Bug," says Potts. "And one of the best techniques involves fishing it shallow, making it dig up the bottom and then letting it rise all the way to the surface before cranking it back down. When most guys are throwing spinnerbaits or supershallow crankbaits, I pick up the Mud-Bug."

Potts has enjoyed good success with the Mud-Bug during the spawn, when he fishes it in bedding areas where the water is too muddy for sight fishing. He also catches a substantial number of cruising bass on the lure in clear water during spring.

Targeting flats or shelves with sandy or muddy bottoms seems to be a key to shallow fishing with the Mud-Bug, he believes.

METAL-LIPPED crankbaits share a common characteristic of imparting a slow, wide wobble that is irresistible to bass.

of the Original Bomber design, but it has more of a crawfish-looking head (complete with bulging eyes). Like the Bomber, it is pulled backward through the water — giving it the appearance of a crawfish darting along the lake bottom in a defensive posture.

• The Heddon Hellbender is a larger lure that differs from the Mud-Bug and Bomber in that the line tie is positioned at the head of the bait. The original Hellbenders sported a small spinner on the tail.

METAL ASSETS

All of these metal-lipped crankbaits share the common characteristics of being fat-bodied and having a slow, wide wobble upon retrieve. Both are attributes that obviously appeal to bass.

Also, they are among the most weedless crankbaits known to man. When they come into contact with objects, their stout metal bills tend to flip the buoyant baits over most danger points. In fact, when one of these lures becomes snagged, it is often because its lip has become wedged under a piece of cover (slack line will almost always free it).

Some fishermen believe there is an added advantage to the baits with metal lips in that they reflect sunlight and give off a flash similar to that of a baitfish.

"Something today's fishermen probably don't realize is that the metal lip is a lot more sensitive than a plastic lip," says Jones, who owns a case of hard-to-find Mud-Bugs with metal bills. "If I need to cover a river ledge and want to find out where the stumps are and what else is down there, I can feel it better with a metal lip than I can with a plastic-lipped crankbait.

"That metal lip is also excellent for dredging the bottom. You can dredge the bottom with a plastic lip, too, but the metal lip produces a sharper shock when it bangs into something, and it sends more of a vibration up the line. Not only are you going to feel more, but that metal lip causes a lot more commotion on the bottom. When

THE DEFLECTING qualities of the wide-billed Mud-Bug are an asset in standing timber. In stumps, the long bill of a Hellbender keeps it more snag free.

you're dredging with that Mud-Bug, it absolutely looks like a crawfish trying its best to get away from something. And the noise it makes does the same thing a rattle does — it helps the fish find the bait. A bass cannot ignore the sound and sight of a Mud-Bug dredging the bottom."

Menendez emphasizes that the bottom-dragging commotion and erratic action inherent in metal-tipped crankers make them best suited for fishing in dingy water.

METAL TARGETS

In terms of depth, Menendez relies on the Bomber in water 5 feet or less; the Mud-Bug gets the call for 6- to 10-foot depths; and he switches to a Hellbender for working 11 to 15 feet.

"Most of my Mud-Bug targets I can see," Klein adds. "Just like fishing a spinnerbait."

A major reason the metal-lipped divers retain a role in the tackleboxes of top pros is the fact that they may be the best heavy cover crankbaits of all.

"The Mud-Bug is one of the best timber baits ever made," Klein continues. "Both hooks are on the belly and away from the front lip. I throw it on 30-pound-test Berkley FireLine, and it crawls through the timber better than any crankbait. I still fish it a lot for big fish in timber, because it will easily come over a branch or walk down a log. I like to fish the larger logs, which don't have so many branches."

Looper emphasizes that many fishermen still troll metal-lipped crankers through flooded timber.

SEASONAL METAL

These lures are most productive from spring through fall, according to Menendez.

"They work great early in the spring, when bass are hanging around stumps, and late in the fall, when the fish can be found ultrashallow in the back ends of creeks," he advises. "I like throwing the Bomber around stumps and working it relatively fast.

"The Mud-Bug is better suited for timber — either standing or laydown timber. It has a lot of wobble, and it kicks out around the timber. I like to work it almost like a worm and finesse it around the cover. I let it float up and over each limb, then I hit the next limb with it and let it suspend temporarily before it begins to float up.

"The Hellbender is best for very heavy stumpy areas on dropoffs. I particularly like that bait in the summertime, when the bass are out on the main river channels and the bass are feeding on shad. I crank it down to the bottom and work it slowly. That heavy metal lip keeps it down, working at a 45 degree angle as you bring it along."

According to Jones, prime time for these unusual crankbaits is the heat of the summer, when the bass are relating to main lake structure. Fishing river ledges in Toledo Bend Reservoir, he has enjoyed success by working a Mud-Bug along the top side of ledges that drop from 10 to 50 feet.

The Color Of Metal

Fans of metal-lipped crankbaits have some definite ideas regarding color combinations of these baits.

Chad Potts, who fishes both the midsize and larger Mud-Bugs in 1 to 4 feet of water, prefers dark red for Texas' grassy lakes. Fellow Texan Alton Jones prefers a crawfish pattern that combines light brown and a hunter green back. Meanwhile, in Kentucky, Mark Menendez' most productive colors are white, solid chartreuse and Christmas tree (white with green stripes and silver flake). And the legendary Bill Dance says, "Over the years, I have caught the living starch out of bass on a black Mud-Bug and a black Bomber."

SHALLOW CRANKING

Finessing And Power Fishing
In Skinny Water With Big
And Small Crankbaits …

A SHALLOW diving crankbait is a great tool for catching bass living year-round in shallow water.

SUPERSHALLOW CRANKS

Deep divers get all the attention, but these skinny-water crankbaits pay dividends throughout the year

A MILD WINTER HAS GIVEN WAY to full-blown cold weather. There is ice in select pockets of the small watershed lake in the Memphis area where Bill Dance has launched his boat.

The warmest water he can find is 38.4 degrees.

It is a morning much better suited for sipping hot coffee than hunting for hot fishing action. But Dance won't be dissuaded. This man truly loves to fish.

It seems that America's television fishing hero has spent too much time exposed to the elements. Dance only fuels such skepticism by tying on a Strike King Scout, a small shallow running crankbait designed to run 12 to 36 inches below the surface. The water is skimmed with ice and this guy is rigging up a surface-hugging crankbait?

Within minutes, the Tennessee angler demonstrates why he was once one of the country's top tournament competitors. Incredibly, he quickly begins catching bass on his Scout.

(Opposite page) BILL DANCE caught this 6-pounder by cranking lily pad stems in January, lending proof that small crankbaits are year-round fish catchers.

By cranking the stems of dead lily pads in 1 to 4 feet of water, Dance boats seven bass topping 2 1/2 pounds, including a 6 1/2-pound ice-water beauty. That was Sunday morning.

On Monday, he returned to the same bitterly cold conditions to catch 16 bass between 2 1/2 and 7 1/2 pounds — all by slowly cranking that Scout with a methodical, even boring routine of three cranks and a pause.

"I have to admit, this surprises even me," Dance says. "I knew this was a great little bait and that cranking shallow water is a good way to catch fish year-round, but

Crankbait Tip

Supershallow crankbaits are especially suited for fishing over matted grassbeds growing near the surface. You can manipulate the bait over the grass with the rod tip and prevent it from hanging up. If the bait catches in the weeds, an abrupt rip with the rod often pops it free to resume its strike provoking wobble.

When shallow cranking, Rick Clunn stays in the Norman N family — Tiny N, Deep Tiny N, Deep Baby N and Big N. Kenyon Hill utilizes a variety of shallow crankers, including the Big N, Bagley's Balsa B3 and Cordell's Big O (in small and medium sizes). All are buoyant and contain rattles.

"The key is choosing the right kind of crankbait for this type of fishing," Kenyon Hill emphasizes. "Not just any crankbait will do. You need to have a very buoyant bait that will float up over the logs when you stop reeling. Most importantly, it needs to have a square lip.

"Baits with square lips will allow you to work the cover better than ones with round or pointed lips. With a rounded lip, the bait might roll over when it strikes an object and gets hung up. But a squared-off lip won't snag nearly as much.

"And you can fish these baits on 20- to 30-pound-test line. That's important because it allows you to drag fish out of some bad places. And when you're talking about cranking shallow cover, you're talking pure meat fishing."

Not to mention pure fun.

these are hardly the ideal conditions for a crankbait."

Dance has long been a fan of shallow cranking, a tactic that has quietly paid off for some of the nation's top tournament pros in recent years. These full-time fishermen know that at least some shallow bass are available throughout the year, and they understand the attributes of diving plugs that stay within 5 feet of the surface. They score handsomely by cranking a depth range most fishermen ignore with crankbaits.

A BIG CRANK'S LITTLE COUSIN

The class of crankbaits recognized by the pros for producing in the shallows would include: Norman's Big N, Mann's 1-Minus, Bomber's 3A, Norman's Tennessee Kil'R, Cordell's Big O, Rebel's Wee R, Storm's Short Wart, Strike King's Scout and Series 1, Bomber's Fat A, Norman's Crappie Crankbait, Excalibur's Swim'N Image and Bandit's Series 101.

"These shallow crankbaits are surprisingly versatile," says Oklahoma's Kenyon Hill. "I consider shallow cranking to be anywhere from a foot to 3 feet, but that doesn't mean you can only use them where the bottom is that deep. You can use the same shallow baits and techniques to catch fish suspended in the tops of trees over deep water. It may be 15 feet to the bottom, but the bass are hanging in the tops of the trees in 3 feet of water,

and you can make them bite by ricocheting your bait off of those limbs."

In addition to diving less than 5 feet during a retrieve, these shallow crankers have other common characteristics that make them reliable bass-catchers in a variety of conditions and seasons.

Many are shallower versions of bigger, deeper crankbaits and sport both the wiggle and bulk of their larger cousins. All feature a small lip and enough buoyancy to float at rest. That same buoyancy, found in the more rotund designs, allows these lures to be worked slowly, and they will swim through cover with surprising ease.

A major attribute is that, as a group, shallow diving crankbaits run at a more precise depth than larger divers, which enables fishermen to work cover more efficiently.

"These shallow divers work so well because they cover a lot of water, and they're always in the strike zone," explains four time world champion Rick Clunn, a cranking expert who has won an untold amount of money on a tiny Norman Crappie Crankbait, which weighs 1/8 ounce and measures 1 1/2 inches. "It's not like trying to reach a very marginal zone down there at 15 feet with a deep running crankbait. It's hard to get a bait that far down and keep it there.

"But when you're cranking shallow water, you can keep the bait in the strike zone all the time."

SHALLOW CRANKING DEFINED

Clunn notes that many who try shallow cranking make the mistake of avoiding cover.

"Shallow water cover is where you'll find the fish," Clunn says. "This is basically spinnerbait fishing with a crankbait. To be successful, you have to throw it in the same places you would a spinnerbait. If you'll do that — when everybody else on the lake is throwing a spinnerbait — you can come behind them and catch fish on a crankbait."

Hill takes Clunn's strategy a step farther. He even cranks shallow cover so dense that most anglers would approach it only with a pitching rod and worm or jig.

The primary criterion for supershallow cranking involves water clarity, according to Clunn. This technique is most productive in stained to muddy water. The off-color conditions keep some resident bass in the shallows throughout the year.

"It depends on what part of the country you live in, but in the South, there's usually some shallow water cranking available year-round," Clunn continues. "With the right water color, some bass will be shallow."

WHEN TO MOVE SHALLOW

Although Hill catches plenty of shallow bass by cranking laydowns and stumps in spring, his favorite seasons for this technique are summer and fall. From June through October, there is an abundance of off-colored water in the lakes he fishes. To his way of thinking, it doesn't matter what the thermometer shows.

"It really can't be too hot," he says. "On those summer days in Oklahoma, we'll have almost 100 degree surface temperature in the dog days of summer. And you can still catch them pretty strong by ricocheting a shallow crankbait through the cover."

Fellow Oklahoma pro O.T. Fears agrees. When the water is at its warmest, he theorizes that shallow bass are most attracted to a big bodied, wide wobbling cranker like his favorite shallow diver — Norman's Big N.

"David Fritts and a few others have developed a reputation for using big crankbaits in deep water, and fishermen have figured out that big crankbaits will work in a lot of different situations, especially in summer," says Fears. "I tend to fish crankbaits in real shallow, heavy cover in less than 5 feet of water, particularly in lakes in Oklahoma and the Arkansas River system."

During the hottest months, pros like Clunn, Fritts and Kevin VanDam rely on shallow running, flat-sided wooden crankbaits, which feature a slender profile, small lip and fairly tight wobbling action that emits plenty of vibration. The four-cornered lips on these lures make them surprisingly weedless.

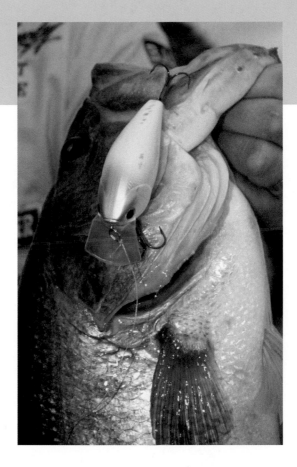

TO BE SUCCESSFUL with shallow crankbaits, you must throw them in harm's way. The key to avoiding hang-ups is a slow retrieve.

Early in the fall, Hill prefers to downsize his shallow crankbaits, switching to a diminutive ultralight Bagley Honey B on light line and a spinning rod to match the hatch of shad fry (which will be about an inch in length). As the water starts to cool later in the season, he returns to big bodied, square-lipped shallow divers, like the Big N, to imitate larger shad that cruise the banks in schools.

World champion Jay Yelas throws a Storm Short Wart in skinny water to solve the postspawn puzzle each year.

Mann's 1-Minus, a fat bodied plug that couldn't run deeper than 12 inches without an anchor tied to it, is one of the more renowned shallow divers. And it is at its best during February and March, when fished around shallow stumps and logs in search of big prespawn bass, according to past Classic champion and cranking authority Paul Elias.

Perinnially consistent pro Mark Davis is a big fan of the Excalibur Shad-R during the prespawn period, when the water temperature is 45 to 52 degrees. "I like the bait's tight action and profile, which are ideal for clear, cold water," Davis says. "The suspending version of the Shad-R really seems to draw those sluggish bass out of the cover."

CRANKING SHALLOW WITH TIM HORTON
Tips from an expert

THE PROS KNOW that mastering all aspects of a certain technique is a key to versatility. And Tim Horton is a big believer in being skilled at cranking in shallow water. Horton was fortunate to have Tennessee River impoundments like Pickwick, Wilson and Wheeler lakes as his classroom for plying the trade. The setting is appropriate, considering the shallow ledges and bars that line the river channel.

First and foremost, stained water is always a bonus in shallow situations, since it forces bass to relate closer to the cover. In clear water conditions, observes Horton, fish will be more prone to cruise or roam their territory, making target-oriented casts less productive.

When an angler finds stained water in backwater areas, the bass will be positioned more predictably around cover. And what makes these

Burning The Shallows

Bass are often shallow for one reason: to feed. If baitfish are seen flipping on the surface in shallow areas and bass are striking at the surface around and among them but won't strike a surface lure, then "burn" a diving crankbait by reeling it extremely fast so it roots bottom and glances off shallow cover. Bass often react immediately to this superfast presentation, which works especially well in early fall.

zones especially good for those willing to seek them out are the fewer places that require one's attention.

"You can be successful in these places because you only need to concentrate on the objects — stickups, laydowns and such," Horton says. "Too often, though, fishermen will see maybe 15 targets and only make one or two casts to each one. Sometimes your first cast will actually run the fish off! I don't know if they eventually get comfortable with the bait coming through their areas or they get mad at it, but one of the two happens. At times, 10 or 15 casts are required to trigger a strike."

Of course, the trick is not to make 10 or 15 haphazard presentations, or presentations that are overly repetitive. To Horton, it's all about angles. Whether he's after bedding fish in the spring or bass that have moved up the creeks in the fall, presenting a crankbait from various angles gives the lure an opportunity to strike the cover from different directions and deflect or carom erratically.

An observant fisherman will pay attention to every cast. When a strike does occur, he has a very precise mental picture of what lure action triggered the response. This is the bedrock of pattern fishing, the very core of developing shallow crankbait strategies.

"For example, when I'm fishing something like willows, I'll pick out the thickest limb that goes to the bottom," advises Horton. "Then, when I generate a strike, I'll know not only where the fish was positioned, but also the angle of the cast and the speed of retrieve that is necessary.

"When the pattern is strong, you get to where you can pull up on a tree and almost pinpoint where the fish is located."

Although retrieve speeds can vary dramatically with each situation, shallow cover often demands a fairly slow and deliberate pace. This is especially true in highly pressured situations in which bass are not particularly aggressive. Under these conditions, Horton casts his crankbait just past the target area whenever possible and brings it past the fish to produce a true reaction bite.

"I want the fish to turn and react to the bait before it knows what happened," he explains.

A critical factor in making these shallow strategies more efficient is choosing a crankbait that fits the cover. To Horton, square- or coffin-shaped lips seem to deflect better off limbs than do rounded ones.

However, he is quick to advise anglers that the greatest limiting factor to success in shallow water is the general unwillingness of anglers to keep moving even shallower.

Precision Cranking With Fritts

One ability that separates crankbait master David Fritts from others is the precision with which he works a submerged stump, rock, brushpile or tree with a crankbait.

It begins with making the perfect cast to set up the proper angle of retrieve. That usually requires making a lengthy cast at a target the size of a bushel basket — which isn't marked. As the lure swims, Fritts tries to visualize the terrain beneath the water and what his lure is doing at all times.

"I always start with a medium retrieve," he says. "Always. No matter the time of year or how cold the water. Then I concentrate on varying the action of the retrieve when I'm getting in the strike zone or where I think the fish are.

"Most of the time, I am slowing it down and speeding it up on the same retrieve. Sometimes I twitch my rod, or just raise it. I often slow the retrieve and raise the rod when the bait approaches the strike zone — because I know it's getting close to the structure, and I want to be ready to set the hook. That sometimes triggers strikes. To consistently get strikes while cranking, you must vary your retrieve."

Crankbait Tip

Crankbaits are highly effective during the prespawn. Bass often move up in large groups to the first breakline, such as a 12-foot flat, close to deep water. There they may hold or "stage," often suspending over the dropoff until conditions are right for spawning.

THE WIDER wobble of a big crankbait transmits a unique sound that triggers the predator instinct of bass in shallow water.

DEEP CRANKING SHALLOW WATER

The pros have found that deep running plugs churn the bottom and stir up big bass

IT SOUNDS LIKE a contradiction in terms — deep diving crankbaits and shallow water structure.

It might seem like bear hunting with a bazooka, a bit overwhelming. And the mere thought of tossing $5 or $6 crankbaits into shal-

low, junglelike cover is enough to scare most anglers into changing tactics.

As bizarre as it might seem, fishing big-lipped, deep diving plugs in shallow water has become standard fare for a growing number of tournament pros and knowledgeable guides who have found it

to be a deadly combination in certain situations.

Sometimes in bass fishing, bizarre makes sense. And this is one of those cases.

"Big, fat deep divers are not limited to deep structure," reveals Arkansas' Rob Kilby. "We've seen a change in how fishermen approach shallow structure and cover, and I would guess this change was born out of competition. With a lot of competition for the same fish, you have to try new things. And sometimes it really works."

These anglers have discovered the special allure of dragging crankbaits made to swim at 10- to 30-foot depths through water as shallow as 2 to 5 feet. And their success makes a good case for the strange combination of deep cranking skinny water.

The pros in the know say this strange fusion offers several advantages.

DIGGING DIRT

Kilby, who scores consistently with a white Bagley DB3 in shallow situations, likes the "different look" it provides. "The wider wobble of these fat-bodied baits creates a different vibration, so the fish see a different sight and (detect) a different sound than they're used to.

"For example, when a spinnerbait tracks through a bush, it has a fairly level an as it comes to you. But a big crankbait comes along, digging up the bottom and creating a mud trail before it hits the bottom of the bush. That is something the fish are not accustomed to, and they will just knock the daylights out of that crankbait."

A major appeal of these lures in shallow water is

the dredging action of the crankbait's broad lip, according to former world champion and cranking expert Paul Elias. Designed to reach far greater depths, a Mann's 20+ or 30+ quickly "overpowers" the shallow water and begins digging up the bottom in the first few turns of the reel handle.

"I think the commotion of the bait digging up the bottom, stirring up the dirt similar to crawfish, is a big attraction," Elias explains. "Plus, I like noise from rattles in a crankbait. The combination of the two gives it the sound and look of a crawfish."

"In crankbait fishing, it is very important that your bait keeps contact with bottom," adds Florida pro Steve Daniel. "That's especially true with cranking shallow water with these deep divers."

FISHING FEARLESSLY

Kilby actually cranks through shallow brush and treetops so thick that it is impossible to get a spinnerbait down to its trunk. With a big crankbait, he casts past the brush, cranks it down to the bottom of the structure and then finesses it through the limbs on its way up.

"The only way most fishermen have to get a lure to the trunk of a tree or base of the brush in some situations is to flip a plastic lure down inside it," Kilby says. "But in clear water situations, you will spook a lot of fish by getting that close. A deep diving crankbait will actually work itself

Crankbait Tips

Big crankbaits provide an edge in shallow water compared to commonly used lures, like worms, jigs and spinnerbaits. They are more likely to attract strikes in the "dead" or coverless water that lies between the boat and bank or between boat docks on a shoreline, for example. Obviously, there are some limits to this unusual technique. The minimum depth in which a deep diving plug can maintain its proper action is about 4 feet, according to the pros, who most often utilize this tactic in 5 to 10 feet of water.

possible on its way back to the boat, he says. That erratic action triggers some vicious strikes.

Daniel finds deep divers to be excellent tools for pulling bass from trees that have fallen in due to erosion along lake- and riverbanks. He makes a short pitch to the tree, cranks the lure down until it makes contact, then gives it momentary slack to allow it to rise. He repeats the process until he clears the end of the tree.

CRANK DEEP, FISH SHALLOW

Although Elias displays the touch of a surgeon when cranking trees and brush, some of his greatest success with the deep cranking/shallow water technique has come while fishing ledges during low water conditions in reservoirs like Lake Eufaula on the Alabama-Georgia border. With the tops of these ledges in 5 to 8 feet of water, Elias uses a Mann's 20+ to burrow along the shallow side before plummeting into the deeper water.

The sight of that big, fat lure digging along the top of the ledge and then suddenly darting off the edge is usually too much for nearby bass to resist.

In several lakes, including Guntersville, Elias has enjoyed good success by what he calls "overpowering the rocks." That involves using a fast retrieve to bounce a Mann's 20+ off a rock-laden bottom in 8 to 10 feet of water. Again, the erratic movement of the crankbait caroming off the rocks triggers an aggressive response from bass in the vicinity.

Although these lures are anything but weedless, the innovative pros have found applications for deep diving crankbaits in shallow water vegetation.

With Sam Rayburn Reservoir well above its normal pool one spring, Elias found he could use a deep diving plug to take advantage of an inside hydrilla line in about 8 feet of water that held big bass. He cast parallel to the edge where grass stopped growing, allowing the lure to dig a path along the sandy bottom.

For working deep running crankbaits in the shallow cover, Daniel prefers lures made of balsa. Balsa offers more buoyancy than plastic or cedar

IN CLEAR WATER conditions, casting a big crankbait can be an asset when flipping and pitching plastic baits spooks the fish, believes Steve Daniel.

behind the base of the structure and then come up through it.

"A lot of people wouldn't think of throwing a crankbait into a tree or buckbrush. But it's really not that difficult with these big-lipped baits. You tend to hang up more with a shallow running crankbait than you do with a deep diving bait, which has a big bill that acts as a weedguard to keep it from hanging up. It comes through the brush with its nose tilted down, which keeps the hooks up and out of line with the limbs. As you bring it through the tree limbs and the bill catches on something, you just pause to let the bait float up, then you continue the retrieve."

Kilby is fearless with these buoyant baits. He often fishes logjams in shallow water in the Arkansas River. The idea is to cast between the logs and allow the lure to careen off everything

baits, he believes, which is a key element in being able to work a diving plug through brush and limbs. Kilby says plastic baits are fine for cranking rocks or sandbanks, but wood is superior in cover.

TACKLING THE BAIT

Great consideration should be given to selecting the proper size for deep cranking in shallow water, according to Daniel.

"Line size really makes a difference in how these baits run," he emphasizes. "You can tie a big crankbait to 30-pound-test line and it won't run over 5 or 6 feet deep. Yet you don't want to throw a crankbait into a tree when you're using 10-pound-test line, because you won't be able to get a bass out of there. So it is important to pick line size based on both the cover and the depth you want to work."

Since much of this technique involves finessing crankbaits through cover, choosing the proper rod is also critical. The rod must have a fairly flexible tip that lets you feel it when the crankbait makes contact. Elias and Daniel like 7-foot rods; Elias favoring the sensitivity of graphite, and Daniel preferring slower responding fiberglass.

While Kilby, Elias, Daniel and Bitter have their favorite brands, other pros practice the technique with deep divers — like Bill Norman's almost indestructible DD 22, Luhr-Jensen's wide-bill Hot Lips Express, Storm's Mag Wart, metal-lipped plugs, like Arbogast's Mud-Bug and various deep running Bomber, Rebel, Normark and Poe's crankbaits.

Although the sight of one of those big crankbaits churning up the bottom attracts plenty of attention, it can also put the angler at a disadvantage at times.

"The only drawback to this type of fishing is that while your bait is digging in the bottom, a lot of times the bass comes down on top of the bait and doesn't get the hooks as well as it would normally," Elias says. "But it triggers a lot of strikes that a smaller crankbait doesn't."

That is a small price to pay when you consider the new arena opened up by the unlikely combination of deep diving crankbaits and shallow water cover. It's a foreign concept that has a growing legion of believers.

Getting The Hang Of It

Part of the challenge of cranking big-lipped baits in shallow water is their susceptibility to get hung up. The risks are obviously worth it, especially if you follow these simple pointers when your crankbait hangs on a limb or stump.

■ Tighten up the line, thrust the rod into the water as far as possible and shake it.
■ Move the rod to the opposite side of the structure and jerk it several times.
■ Finally, drop a lure retriever down the line, and it will usually knock the plug loose on the initial drop. More stubborn hang-ups require bouncing the retriever up and down a few times.

TYING A big crankbait to heavy line enables it to run through the preferred strike zone in shallow water.

CRANK THE BANK FOR BRONZEBACKS

In rivers and tailraces, diving baits slice the current and hook quality bronzebacks

COMPARED TO JIGS, spinnerbaits, jerkbaits, topwater plugs and a variety of soft plastic offerings, crankbaits get relatively little attention from many smallmouth anglers. But when brown bass hug the bank, especially a shoreline swept by current, crankbaits deserve a high priority.

No one knows this better than John Schwarzel, who scores well on smallmouth with crankbaits when he fishes bass tournaments on the Ohio River.

There's plenty to talk about regarding the Ohio nowadays. Despite the abysmal largemouth fishing during the latter half of the 1990s, the river's smallmouth bass are suddenly on the upswing. So much so, in fact, they are showing up in substantial numbers farther south on the Ohio than ever before.

"Zebra mussels have taken hold on the Ohio River," says Schwarzel. "They've cleared up the water, and that may be part of the reason we're seeing more smallmouth. I also think smallmouth are benefiting from more stringent efforts to prevent chemical spills from industrial plants along the river. Those spills take a heavy toll on bass."

While his experience for cranking shoreline smallies is based on the Ohio, anglers elsewhere can apply Schwarzel's expertise on other rivers.

THE CURRENT EQUATION

(Opposite page) FIND SUCCESS for river bronzebacks by targeting natural or man-made current breaks located along the shoreline.

According to Schwarzel, the most important factor for catching smallmouth on crankbaits is current. When the water runs swift, it creates eddies

Crankbait Tips

Smallmouth congregate at shoals formed at the mouths of washes. The bass may locate behind the shoal, at the point of the shoal and along the upstream edge. When the fish hold upstream, they are usually feeding most aggressively and can be caught on a crankbait.

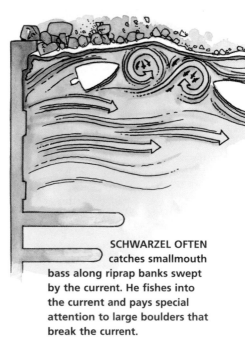

ONE PRIMARY SPOT for smallmouth is where the downstream current from the dam turns into the bank and splits, with part of the current curling back upstream. Smallmouth hold in the eddy on the edge of the fast water. Typically, John Schwarzel alternately positions the boat upstream and downstream from an eddy to work it from both angles. Bear in mind that a portion of the eddy flows upstream against the bank for some distance before being picked up by the air current.

SCHWARZEL OFTEN catches smallmouth bass along riprap banks swept by the current. He fishes into the current and pays special attention to large boulders that break the current.

and current breaks along the bank that provide niches where smallmouth may duck out of the flow and nab shad and other forage being washed to them.

The most consistent current occurs just downstream from the navigation dams along the Ohio River, and these are the areas where crankbaits most often produce smallmouth for Schwarzel.

One primary spot for smallmouth is where the downstream current from the dam turns into the bank and splits, with part of the current curling back upstream. Smallmouth hold in the eddy on the edge of the fast water.

"It's not hard to figure where smallmouth are likely to be, once you get the hang of it," says Schwarzel. "In fact, I've fished tournaments where I've caught smallmouth all day from a 30-yard stretch of bank."

Exactly where Schwarzel positions his boat and casts his crankbaits depends on the shape and motion of the eddy. Because smallmouth face into the flow when feeding, Schwarzel retrieves a crankbait with the current whenever possible. In many instances, he'll alternately position the boat upstream and downstream from an eddy to work it from both angles. Bear in mind that a portion of the eddy flows upstream against the bank for some distance before being picked up by the main current.

"Sometimes the bass will be tight to the bank, which is typically covered with riprap below most dams," says Schwarzel. "But they also may be out away from the bank, feeding along the edge where the main current meets the eddy."

Schwarzel also fares well fishing crankbaits parallel to riprap banks brushed by the current. Any large boulder that sticks out farther than the rest of the rocks is an optimum target, and it frequently produces more than one bass.

SMALLMOUTH STRATEGIES

On the Ohio River, crankbaits yield more smallmouth in the spring and fall. During the summer, the current slows, and the bass scatter and go deeper. But even in the summertime, an increase in the current pulls the bass shallow.

Other key smallmouth locations for Schwarzel include rock and gravel piles formed near dams by dredging operations. Gravel bars that form at the mouths of washes also produce bass. When fishing bars, Schwarzel generally positions his boat downstream from the structure and fan casts it. Depending on the current, the bass may hold on the backside of the bar, up on the bar, on the tip of the bar, or along the upstream edge of the bar. They assume the latter position when feeding aggressively.

The heads of islands typically have long gravel points that divert the current and create an eddy, as well as current breaks along each side of the island. If stumps are present on the point, bass duck behind them when feeding. Bump a crankbait around a stump in the current, and you'll often trigger a jolting strike.

Outside river bends are usually swept by stronger currents than straight banks and inside bends. Schwarzel gives such places a lot of attention when current flows are low, particularly outside bends embellished by stumps and boulders that provide smallmouth with current breaks.

Smallmouth regularly congregate in the mouths of tributaries, where eddies form during strong current flows. Schwarzel frequently eases his boat into the mouth of the

Tackle For Brown Fish

The smaller sizes of the Big O and the Model 200 Bandit account for many of John Schwarzel's smallmouth bass. Concentrating on depths of less than 6 feet when cranking in current, he regularly bounces bottom with the lures and works them with an aggressive stop-and-go action as they swim free above bottom. Firetiger and pearl/chartreuse back are two proven colors.

Schwarzel slings crankbaits with a No. 4 action 6-foot, 6-inch, Falcon graphite baitcasting rod and 10-pound Izor line. The rod is limber enough in the tip to be forgiving with treble hooks, yet it has plenty of backbone for long casts and battling heavy smallmouth.

"A lot of guys use glass rods when fishing crankbaits," says Schwarzel. "I prefer the sensitivity of graphite because it helps me feel when a crankbait comes through a change in the current, say, from fast water into an eddy, or vice versa. I immediately feel the sudden surge of a strong current or when the tug of the current slacks off. That tells me my crankbait is in the strike zone and to stop cranking momentarily."

The graphite rod also helps Schwarzel distinguish whether the bottom is mud, sand, rock or gravel, and when the bottom composition changes from one substance to another. Such transition areas also hold smallmouth.

creek, casts out into main current and runs his crankbaits through the edge that separates the fast water from the eddy.

The points that form on either side of the creek mouth also attract smallmouth, he says.

CRANKING THE CREEKS

Creek mouths on the lower pools of the Ohio River are no strangers to Kentucky pro Mark Menendez.

"In my part of the Ohio River (the Paducah area), the upstream mouth of a creek usually has a flat built up on it," says Menendez. "If I can find some rock on the up-current side, that's where I tend to catch smallmouth. I usually cast the crankbait upstream and bring it back downstream. That's a more natural presentation.

"I like to rip crankbaits over cover for smallmouth," says Menendez. "I always watch my bait coming in as I'm preparing to make the next cast. Smallmouth are notorious for 'tailgating' a bait but not biting it. If I see one or two follows, I'll start an inconsistent stop-and-go retrieve that resembles a car with carburetor problems choking down the road."

Another ploy that pays off for Menendez is to sweep the crankbait ahead several feet when he feels it break free from the bottom.

TAILRACE SMALLIES

These tactics also pay off with quality smallmouth bass when Menendez fishes the Kentucky River below Kentucky Dam. Many of the better spots are overlooked because the adjacent banks are comprised of mud. Riprap areas are fished hard, but they produce far more largemouth than smallmouth.

"If you can find a little isolated patch of rock that sticks out far enough into the river to create a feeding shelf and an eddy, you've found the magic formula for some awfully big smallmouth," says Menendez.

Most of these natural rock formations extend into the river less than 30 yards. Rocks on the bank often provide a tip-off to the shelves, but not always. The ability to read the water and see the eddies will put you on rarely fished hot spots.

"You may have a flat 4 to 8 feet deep that immediately falls off into 10 to 12 feet," says Menendez. "The bass hang right on that lip most of the time, particularly if there's a big rock or a snag there that breaks the current."

Menendez positions his boat downstream just off the end of the point and casts his crankbaits upstream at about a 45 degree angle. Once he's located the sweet spot that holds the bass, he cuts his casting angle to about 30 degrees so he can run the lure through the fish more precisely.

"The current is dictated by the release of water below the dam," says Menendez, "and it relates directly to how much electricity they're generating. In the hot summertime, when people are running air conditioners, there's a lot of current most of the time. That makes smallmouth easier to find. If there's no current whatsoever, you don't catch many brown fish."

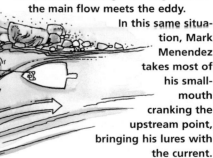

EDDIES FORM in creek mouths during strong flows. Schwarzel positions his boat inside the creek mouth and runs his crankbait through the edge where the main flow meets the eddy.

In this same situation, Mark Menendez takes most of his smallmouth cranking the upstream point, bringing his lures with the current.

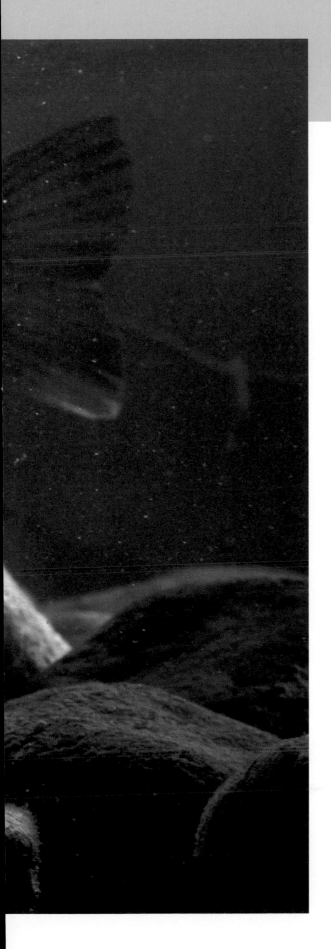

DEEP CRANKING

Learning The Nuances
Of The Most Effective
Lure For Deep Water …

DEEP CRANKING is not the arm-straining technique that it once was, thanks to crankbaits made for this productive method.

SECRETS OF DEEP CRANKING
New tricks from the innovator of deep cranking

PAUL ELIAS' NAME IS SYNONYMOUS with deep cranking, dating back to the time when he won a BASS world championship title in the early 1980s. Since then, the crankbait expert has designed lures and refined techniques that are popular in mainstream bass fishing.

Elias' most notable victory spawned a technique called "kneeling and reeling," for no other reason than crankbaits running in the double digit range were a rarity at the time.

Today, crankbaits run up to 20 feet or more, with Elias compelled to redefine the term and technique for which he is well-known.

"Actually, the term 'deep cranking' is not always what people think it is," Elias points out. "Many fishermen think that if you're using a crankbait that runs 20 or 30 feet deep, you have to fish it that deep, but that isn't the case.

"I consider deep cranking anything below 12 feet. The deepest I've ever used a crankbait — a Mann's 30+ — was 24 feet."

In Elias' deep cranking strategy, the primary ingredient is not depth alone, but rather, cover and/or structure located in the proper zone of 12 to about 20 feet.

"You can reduce deep cranking to two simple factors," says Elias. "The first in locating that cover and structure, and the second is getting a crankbait down there. It isn't that mysterious or complicated when you analyze what you're trying to accomplish."

(Opposite page) PAUL ELIAS uses his depthfinder to get a mental picture of what's below the surface. The electronic aid helps him save time while eliminating unproductive areas.

Crankbait Tip

There is mixed opinion among pros on the best lines to use with crankbaits. Many feel that because shock absorption is a primary consideration, braided lines, which have very little stretch, are not highly recommended with crankbaits. These anglers prefer low diameter, abrasion-resistant mono lines testing from 10 to 15 pounds instead. Other pros like low stretch braided lines for cranking; they are willing to sacrifice shock absorption for the enhanced sensitivity these lines afford. Whichever type of line is chosen, remember that the thinner the line's diameter, the less drag it will have in the water and the deeper the lure will go.

Deep Cranking Tackle

Paul Elias has tried a variety of rod actions over the years, and for a time changed to fiberglass rods, but, unlike some of his contemporaries, he doesn't particularly like the limber sticks. He does not believe his own hooking percentage improved with glass, so he went back to graphite.

Today his rod choice is a Quantum Tour Edition 7-footer with a medium-light popping action. The tip is fairly light to enable long casts, but the butt is strong enough to handle any big bass that may hit.

Elias also uses the Quantum EX 300 reel with a slow 4.4:1 ratio. "You want a lower gear ratio for several reasons," he says. "It's certainly easier to use because you don't have to change your natural retrieve speed. The reel does it for you. You can feel the lure better, and actually get it deeper. And because the lure is moving slower, you don't have to fight it as hard."

For line, he uses green Trilene XT in 12-, 14- and 17-pound-test strengths, although he may go as light as 8-pound test for extremely long casting.

"The only other thing I can say about deep cranking is that for some reason chartreuse seems to be the best color for me," Elias adds. "I think it may represent a bluegill to the bass. I have dozens of crankbaits in the boat with me at any given time, and nearly all have at least some chartreuse on them."

WHEN TO CRANK DEEP

"As much as anything, the time of year and the type of lake help me choose a fishing area."

In early summer, for example, with bass migrating out of tributary creeks, Elias starts at the first major bends coming out of the creeks. During the morning hours he likes structure that may be 7 to 10 feet deep but very close to 20-foot water. As the day gets hotter, he moves to deeper structure in 12 to 20 feet.

Later in summer, Elias feels many bass relate more to the main river channel itself, so he concentrates on underwater humps and ridges as well as in the mouths of major tributaries. As summer gives way to fall, Elias moves back into the creeks, since bass are following shad into the creeks that time of year.

"I'm not doing anything radically different," he says, "except that, instead of casting to the shorelines, I'm casting to channels and other structure. In fact, my fishing is a lot like shallow shoreline fishing; even there, you sometimes have to cover a lot of water before you find the bass."

MOST CRANKBAIT fish are lost due to manhandling during the fight. Let the fish tire itself out a safe distance from the boat while keeping the line tight.

The obvious question, of course, is how do you pick that initial tributary creek to begin fishing?

"First, I want a large tributary, because it simply will have more room for more fish," Elias explains. "Next, I want a creek that has a lot of bends and irregularities. I think creeks and even rivers are major highways for bass, and the bends, both inside and outside bends, always seem to have some cover in them. That's all I was fishing when I won the Classic, a major river bend where a lot of brush had washed in.

"I also like a lot of structure in the creek I'm fishing, and this is where map study is very important. I study good lake maps carefully, particularly on waters I haven't fished before. I want as many shallow water/deep water drops as possible."

"Surprisingly, in a lake with a lot of vegetation, you have to actually study the quality and cover of the grass itself when you're looking for fish. If your crankbait constantly digs up dead brown grass or moss, you need to look for a new spot. Bass seem to like healthier, greener vegetation."

In summer, Elias concentrates on sharper dropoffs, because that's where he tends to find larger schools of fish. In the fall, however, he prefers more gradual depth changes.

"I believe bass begin their fall migration back to shallow water creeks soon after the first full moon in August," says Elias. "Often, the first cold front of the year passes through about this time, and when bass decide to move shallow, they can do it in a hurry."

In winter, Elias rates deep cranking a poor second to jigging. The deep diving plugs just are not as efficient in cold weather, partly because most bass are deeper than most crankbaits can work effectively.

MAKING CONTACT

"There is a limit to the effective range of today's crankbaits," explains Elias. "I think the key is to use a big bill lure that gets down quickly and digs along the bottom for as long as possible.

"There is no question you'll get more strikes when the lure is hitting or bouncing off something than you will if it is simply running through the water. My entire game plan is to make the lure look like a real baitfish. When it comes around cover, I pause it, then speed it up so it looks like it's trying to get away."

One of the crucial aspects of deep cranking, says Elias, is learning to feel the lure bumping into cover. You reel until you feel the lip hit something, and then pause so the lure rises. Then you give the plug a quick jump forward to make it look like it is trying to escape from something. That's when the majority of strikes happen.

"A lot of fishermen simply don't fish an area thoroughly enough," Elias continues. "You have to cover a lot of ground and go through a process of elimination. You may fish a quarter-mile of a ledge without a strike, and then suddenly find a school of fish, or you may locate bass bunched at one end of a sandbar and not at the other.

"That's why I do a lot of looking with my depthfinders, trying to get a mental picture of the entire area. I just imagine I'm going down a shoreline but the depthfinder and my crankbait are doing the looking for me.

More Tips For Fishing Deep Divers

■ **Make long casts** — The longer the cast, the more time the lure will spend at the lower reaches of its depth capability. A long, flexible rod with a two-handed grip facilitates longer casts, as does lighter line. A short cast/heavy line may not permit the lure to dive deep enough to reach the fish.

■ **Keep the rod low** — Stand up and point the rod tip at the water when cranking. This enables the lure to dive deeper. Some anglers sink the rod tip — or nearly the entire rod — into the water while "kneeling and reeling;" this gets the lure deep, but shouldn't be necessary with many of today's deep diving lures.

■ **Use a sweep hook set** — When a bass strikes a crankbait, it may be only lightly hooked. A hard, sudden hook set — the kind used with a plastic worm or jig — may rip the hook out of the fish. Instead, with the rod tip low, sweep the rod to the side while reeling quickly. The supersharp hooks used by most crankbait manufacturers today will sink deeper as the fish struggles.

■ **Be patient bringing the fish to the boat** — Most crankbait-hooked bass are lost when the angler gets in too great a hurry and tries to "horse" the fish quickly to the boat. Let the bass fight a safe distance from the boat while maintaining a tight line. Then, as the fish gradually tires, slowly work it to the boat until it's close enough for you to determine where and how well the bass has been hooked.

DAVID FRITTS' CRANKING SEMINAR

A top pro and crankbait master
tells how to get the most out of diving baits

CRANKBAITS ARE GREAT TOOLS for catching bass — probably the best tools in your tacklebox.

But as with any tool, you have to know the best ways to use a crankbait. To me, the most important thing about a crankbait is learning to feel the bait.

A crankbait is similar to a spinnerbait in that both are usually retrieved steadily back to the boat. But unlike a spinnerbait, a crankbait has its own built-in action. Every time it moves, it tells you something. You have to learn what it is telling you with each move it makes.

More often than you might think, a bass hits a crankbait in such a way that you can't feel it. Many people actually don't know when they get bites. Sure, bass sometimes will "commit suicide" on a crankbait, but many times, the bite is a lot more subtle.

Glen Lau's famous video, *Bigmouth*, was an eye-opener for me. In the video, a fisherman is retrieving his crankbait when a giant bass suddenly swims up and sucks the bait in. The fisherman continues winding — without knowing he has a strike. The bass just opens its mouth, and the bait swims right out. I believe this happens often.

COLOR IS KEY

Color gives me a great edge in crankbait fishing.

Here's why: If you happen to hit a bass on the head, you're going to catch it. But the key is to attract fish to your bait. And that begins with color.

When I find the right color, I am able to draw fish from a distance. That means more bites every day. It also means I'll catch a bigger fish every now and then.

Using the right color produces harder strikes, too, so the fish will be hooked better and will be easier to land.

If you pay attention, a fish will tell you whether it really wants the color you're using.

How many times have you wound in a bass that only has the back hook? More than likely, that bass was following the bait and only nipped at it as the lure was starting to swim up.

Other fish might be hooked under the chin or on the side of the head. In this situation, a bass was just knocking the bait, trying to get it out of

SHAD COLORS, crawfish patterns, tricolor hues, chartreuse and otherwise flashy tones are favorites of crankbait guru David Fritts.

its way. In either case, you probably weren't using the best color.

What you want to see is nothing but the crankbait's bill sticking out of a fish's mouth. That means the fish really wanted your crankbait.

Crankbait Tip

To find the level that bass are holding on a point, begin fishing the end of the point, from shallow to deep. Hold the boat in deep water and fish the sharpest breakline of the point, making casts down the spine until you intercept the bass.

Fritts On Crankbait Quirks

Over the years, I have found there are some very subtle differences between crankbaits of the same type, brand and color.

One thing that makes some crankbaits better than others is whether they run true. A bait that always strives to find a center line is a much better fish producer — always. Some brands of crankbaits are more consistent than others, but any bait can get out of tune, and you'll need to know how to adjust it.

A swimming pool is an ideal place to tune crankbaits, since the water is clear enough for you to see your bait as it swims. You want it to come in as perfectly straight as it can. A lure that runs just 4 inches off center can make a difference. If that bait swims to the right, for example, you should bend the line tie very slightly to the left.

A tuned crankbait runs deeper and performs better than one that's slightly out of tune. The effort to tune your baits will make an unbelievable difference in your cranking success.

IN SUMMERTIME, Fritts chooses a solid crankbait instead of a rattling model because the fish are not as aggressive. The subtle approach, he believes, produces more and bigger fish.

A bass that really wants a crankbait will always attack from the front. When the front hook is in its mouth, that's a signal you're using the right color.

PRODUCTIVE WITH CRANKS

In my view, there are five basic color schemes worth trying: tri-color patterns, shad colors, crawfish patterns, chartreuse and other bright, flashy colors.

Crawfish colors are always good in the spring. At that time, bass like to be around rocky structure because rocks warm up from the sun a little more quickly, and rocks attract crawfish.

In the summertime, a green crankbait is one of my favorites. It's a good clear water color because it sort of stands out. Green — ranging from firetiger to lime — crankbaits seem to catch the biggest fish in the area. Often, after I've caught a limit on a blue or shad-colored bait, I'll tie on a green bait and try to catch a big bass.

Another good color in the summer, especially in water that's stained from algae, is something with a blue back. It's a good idea to start with that color in summer.

In cold weather, I use shad-colored baits, but later switch to flashy colors, like chrome or solid white. These colors reflect light similar to a jigging spoon, which is a winter standard.

And then, there's chartreuse, which works any time of the year, especially in summer and fall.

CRANKBAIT DESIGNS

When choosing the best crankbait design for each situation, you have to know something about the action of that bait. For example, whether it has a tight wiggle or a wide wobble.

A bait with a bill that runs perfectly straight into the body will have a tight action. The more slanted the bill, the wider it wobbles.

Wide moving, vibrating baits are always better in shallow water. The bass you find in shallow water usually are a little more aggressive than those in deeper water.

For that reason, you need both styles. If you're fishing in the spring or fall and bass are feeding, you need to throw something that makes a lot of noise and a lot of vibration.

But in summer, when it's tough and you're not getting many bites, you need to go with something more subtle.

I don't like to throw a rattling bait in the summertime. I like to stick with a bait that doesn't make a lot of noise and gets a subtle approach. You'll find you'll catch more fish — and bigger fish — doing that.

Another crankbait you need to have in your tacklebox is a flat-sided crankbait with a "four-corner," or coffin-shaped, lip.

The four-corner crankbait is so effective because it reacts entirely differently from a rounded bill when it contacts an underwater object.

A crankbait with a rounded bill will hit an object and roll, but this style bait does something completely different. Because of the edges on the lip, it can't roll very easily. Instead, it hits the object, backs up and turns.

A MATTER OF DEPTH

Another important aspect of crankbaiting is knowing exactly how deep a crankbait will run. Most people don't realize that the difference between catching a big bass and not getting a bite can be as little as 6 inches. It has happened to me many times.

Let's say you buy a crankbait that, according to the label, runs 15 to 21 feet. But when you fish the bait, it doesn't seem to get quite that deep.

Sound familiar? It may be that your line size is the problem. I use crankbaits on 10-pound-test Stren Sensor line most of the time. That's the optimum choice for achieving maximum depth.

FRITTS OPTS for a fiberglass cranking rod because it's slower than graphite. The resulting benefit is you won't jerk the bait away from the fish on the hook set.

If you go from 10-pound to 8-pound test, you'll gain about 10 inches in depth. But if you size up from 10 to 12 pounds, you'll lose about a foot of depth. And 14-pound line will rob you of another 1 1/2 feet of depth.

CRANKING AT THE NEXT LEVEL

Study these four facets of crankbait fishing to catch bass like a pro

IN ANY SPORT, taking one's game to the next level can be a difficult proposition. In crankbait fishing, it can be especially frustrating, since stepping up in performance not only means understanding the basics, but refining them.

For David Fritts, crankbaiting's top expert, the refinement process is an ongoing obsession — one that keeps him forever dissatisfied with the status quo. Believing that every facet of his crankbaiting program can be improved, this North Carolina pro painstakingly breaks down his crankbait strategy into distinct categories, among them zone, presentation, retrieve and action.

In this breakdown of crankbait technique, he lists them in no particular order of importance. "You can't overlook any of them," remarks Fritts, "because they can all make a difference in your results."

However, the sheer number of crankbaits multiplied by the countless variations in weather and water conditions makes it impossible to create a detailed handbook on what to do and when to do it. Rather, the mastery of crankbaiting comes in recognizing what's important and then refining those items on a daily basis. In fact, if it's possible to say that one lure category demands more on-the-water experimentation than another, crankbaits would most likely be the choice.

IN THE ZONE

At the core of Fritts' crankbait philosophy is recognizing that crankbaits are "zone" lures. In other words, each crankbait delivers a productive strike zone that varies with each cast and every an-gling situation. Even with an extremely long cast, notes Fritts, a crankbait only produces an effective zone of 5 to 15 yards.

"Remember, a crankbait is like a pendulum," he cautions. "It doesn't go to the bottom as soon as it hits the water. Different baits act differently. Some of them dive sharply, while most go down on a slant.

"Once crankbaits reach a certain depth, they inch down from there. That's why long casts are very important."

As a result, the formula is a simple one: The effective zone of a crankbait is expanded with longer casts. This is precisely why Fritts prefers staying out in deeper water and throwing in shallow, so

USE A REEL with a slow gear ratio to make a crankbait run at a constant speed and depth.

the pendulum action of his crankbait is aided by the slope of the bottom contour.

This zone concept is also crucial in covering water, one of the most important advantages to crankbait fishing. By identifying the primary fish-holding depth, choosing the correct lure size and depth capabilities, an angler can then focus only on the depth zones that offer productive structure or cover.

PRESENTATION

"There is no wrong way to present a crankbait," says Fritts. No matter where bass are located, he knows their behavior, and their moods can never be considered stable. That's why getting in a rut with crankbait presentations and using the same cadence repeatedly is counterproductive.

Of the countless choices available, Fritts places great value on a stop-and-go retrieve, in which brief pauses actually produce a more natural look to the presentation. According to Fritts, this presentation makes the lure appear "nervous" to bass, a sure way to generate strikes from opportunistic predators.

Perhaps the most difficult aspect of refining one's presentations is first recognizing all the variables that went into producing a strike and then being able to duplicate them. Paying close attention to every single cast is the key. Unless you're alert to exactly what you are doing when a fish responds to the bait, you'll miss the opportunity to duplicate the retrieve or cadence, and you'll never know how many bass you left behind.

RETRIEVE SPEED

At the heart of any presentation is the speed at which a crankbait is retrieved. Altering that speed alters the presentation, pure and simple. While there are moments when a fast retrieve is desirable, in most cases the object of crankbaiting is to place the lure near the structure or cover and walk the bait through slowly.

Even though fishermen using faster reels (with higher gear ratios) can adjust their cranking speed, it is much easier to produce consistent results with a slower gear ratio. Many times, a small dose of adrenaline — or merely a lapse in concentration — can increase retrieve speed without the angler being aware of it. As a result, Fritts addresses the issue with a mechanical solution: He fishes his crankbaits on a slow reel, a Lew's BB1NG with a 4.3:1 gear ratio.

ACTION

"Every crankbait — even one that looks the same as others — is different in some way or another," notes Fritts, "whether it is in the vibration, the roll or the noise it produces.

"You can actually look at a crankbait and have a pretty good idea what it will do. The angle of the lip, the shape of the lip and the shape of the body — flat or round — dictate the action of the lure."

While Fritts could fill an encyclopedia on the subtle differences between various crankbait brands and styles, the emphasis again is for anglers to understand the performance aspects of the baits they use. To only have a vague notion of a crankbait's strengths and weaknesses is a handicap of the highest order. But in taking the time to assess depth range, wobble characteristics, noise production, ability to move through cover and deflection properties, a fisherman gains confidence and eliminates confusion over which lure best suits the prevailing conditions.

Crankbait Tip

Changing weight and weight distribution is a popular way of improving a crankbait. A favored means of adding weight is by using Storm Lures' adhesive SuspenDots or SuspenStrips. Other crankbaiters wrap lead wire around hooks. More subtle changes, such as swapping out hooks for improved hookup ratios and filing the diving bill for better action, frequently can make a huge difference in your success with crankbaits.

BODY SIZE, water depth and lure action are three criteria Mark Davis uses for choosing a crankbait.

CRANKING DEEP WITH MARK DAVIS

This veteran Arkansas pro reveals the structure secrets that have enabled him to win multiple BASS point titles

STRUCTURE FISHING IS MUCH LIKE A JIGSAW PUZZLE put out in front of you on the table, except in fishing you can't see the pieces. You have to find them first before you can solve the puzzle."

That's how Mark Davis describes structure fishing, the technique that keeps him a perennial contender on the BASS tour, including point championships and a Bassmaster Classic world title.

Davis began learning the secrets of structure fishing when, at age 15, he started guiding on Lake Ouachita in west-central Arkansas. From there he jumped into the pro ranks and quickly established a reputation as one of the tour's premier cranking experts. Through the years, Davis has developed an uncanny knowledge of how to unlock the unseen secrets of ledges, humps, channels and breaklines.

In this interview, the popular Arkansas pro offers his thoughts on things every angler can do to improve his own structure fishing techniques.

BASSMASTER: What is the very first step in structure fishing?
DAVIS: Fishing the proper depth is the absolute key. It's not whether you fish points, channels or humps, but rather that you locate the activity zone fish are using. Once you know that zone, you can locate structure at that depth.
BASSMASTER: What is the activity zone?

(Opposite page) MARK DAVIS always stops on structure points with long, wide flats and sharp breaklines. The steepest, fastest break is where he most often finds the bass.

DAVIS: Every lake has basic depth ranges that bass tend to use during the late spring, the summer and the winter. These are fairly consistent from year to year, too. Normally, you see baitfish rather than

Crankbait Tip:

A crankbait's productive "zone" is the distance it can be retrieved at the proper depth. A shallow diver, for example, reaches its working depth quickly and stays there longer, while a deep diver swims at its maximum depth for a much shorter period.

gamefish as you study your electronics, but there will be a certain depth where you see a lot of activity, and it will be fairly distinct. This is the activity zone.

BASSMASTER: How do you determine this depth?

DAVIS: I use water clarity, the time of year and my electronics to find the activity zone. As I idle across open water, I'll watch the depthfinder closely, and I may cross several large bays or tributaries just looking for baitfish on the depthfinder. Wherever I start fishing, such as on a deeper point, for example, I'll also keep watching my electronics.

BASSMASTER: How does the time of year influence this activity zone?

DAVIS: The time of year influences where bass are likely to be on a lake more than the actual depth they're using. When you're going to fish structure, you can't start looking for structure just anywhere. You must take into account what the bass have been doing and where they have been living. This will help you narrow your search considerably — for both structure and bass.

BASSMASTER: When you determine the depth of the activity zone, you then try to find structure at that depth. Are some types of structure better than others at certain times of the year? Why should you fish a point rather than a ledge, or a channel break instead of a hump?

DAVIS: You have to take what the lake gives you, and every lake is different. Some lakes have more points or better ledges than others, and this is information you can learn from a map.

BASSMASTER: Can you recommend a general starting point on most lakes when you're going to fish structure, regardless of the time of year?

DAVIS: If you don't have any information or ideas where to start, I suggest fishing a flat that has a deep water drop on one side. Anywhere you go, anytime of year, bass love flats. Fish the steepest depth change on that flat.

BASSMASTER: How would you fish such a spot?

DAVIS: First, remember two things about all structure fishing: You have to have the proper mind-set because you're searching, and it may take quite awhile and a lot of casts to find the fish. Second, all you want initially is one bite — just one indication bass are present. Structure bass are school bass, so one bite nearly always indicates you've found a school.

With a flat that I don't know, I have my boat in the deeper water, and I cast parallel to the break, starting the lure up on top of the flat and angling it across the break. This way, the lure stays in the potential strike zone the longest amount of time.

I'm basically casting ahead of the boat, but once I get a bite, I usually move the boat farther out in deeper water to avoid spooking the fish. I change my casting angle, because sometimes just the angle a lure comes through a school of fish is a critical part of the puzzle. If I get two or three bass on successive casts, I may drop a marker buoy, not to mark the bass but to mark my boat position so I can keep that same casting angle.

BASSMASTER: What's your lure choice for this type of fishing?

DAVIS: I want to use a crankbait if the edge of the break is 15 feet or less. I want the crankbait making contact with the bottom, but it does not have to be digging into the bottom, and 15 feet is really just about the maximum depth at which most crankbaits are efficient. Structure bass tend to be in small, tight schools and might only be in an area the size of a boat, or even smaller. You can pinpoint them the easiest with a crankbait, which is what makes them such good lures.

Crankbaits also tend to attract larger bass.

If the structure is too deep for fishing with a

Creek Channel

22'

Creek channel →

25'

13'

12'

Davis works a shoreline by casting ahead of the boat (A). When he locates fish, he positions the boat away from the structure to avoid disturbing the bass (B).

26'

12'

B

A

A

Boat position when hunting bass — casting parallel to the ledge.

13'

28'

If cover (such as stumps) is present, structure can be even more productive. But the features that attract Davis to this spot are the outside bend of the creek and the intersection of a ditch with the creek channel.

DAVIS USES a crankbait on a
breakline when the depth is
15 feet or less.

crankbait, I'll use a Carolina rig with a soft plastic
lizard or worm. I can fish it fast and cover the
water, and it will get a lot of strikes, but usually
from smaller fish.

BASSMASTER: You're known for fishing channel bends. What's your secret there?

DAVIS: Like flats and ledges, channel bends are
good anytime — especially in the summer. I fish
the outside bends first, and I don't even look at the
straight sections. A creek or river with a lot of
bends is never as good as one with only a few
bends. The high percentage spot will be the first
bend after a long, straight section of channel.

I will have my boat in the deep water and cast
at a 45 degree angle upstream and across the bend.
You move slowly around the bend, both with your
boat and your casts, trying to cover the spot from
different angles. I'll even get close to the shoreline
and make parallel casts that way.

BASSMASTER: What about fishing points?

DAVIS: To me, the best structure points are the
long, wide, flat ones that have a good break on one
side or on the end. This actually makes them resemble flats, to some extent. I always fish the
steepest, fastest break first because nine times out
of 10, it will hold the bass.

I keep the activity zone depth in mind, but I
don't limit myself to that level when fishing points.
Most anglers tend to fish structure too shallow, but
I often overcompensate and fish it too deep. For example, if the activity zone is at 20 feet, I start fishing
at 25 feet and work up to 15 feet. I keep my boat in
deep water and cast up on the point and bring my
lure over the top of the point and down the drop.

BASSMASTER: How do you select which
crankbait to use?

DAVIS: I consider four factors: profile or body size,
water depth, lure action and the size of the bass I expect to catch. Basically, in warmer water or for larger
bass, I use a larger lure. In clear water, I will use a
smaller crankbait, and also one that has a tighter,
more natural action. Depthwise, I want a lure that
runs deeper than the depth of the fish; if bass are at
10 feet, I choose a crankbait that dives 12 to 13 feet.

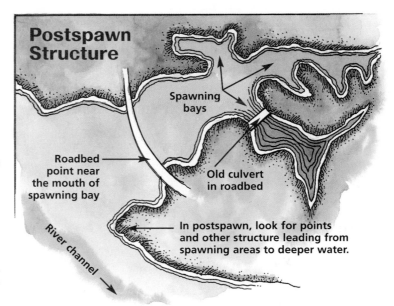

Postspawn Structure

Spawning bays

Roadbed point near the mouth of spawning bay

Old culvert in roadbed

River channel

In postspawn, look for points and other structure leading from spawning areas to deeper water.

BASSMASTER: How long do you fish structure
before you give up and leave?

DAVIS: When I'm fishing the break on the edge
of a flat, I like to fish the entire length of the ledge
or break, because I know how much bass use flats.
Sometimes, this may take an entire day, or longer.
On points, I may just work down to 15 feet, depending on the activity zone depth. Before I leave
any area, I try different lures and use different casting angles.

BASSMASTER: Do active structure bass tend to
bite on every cast?

DAVIS: Yes, they do, once you're dialed into the
right casting angle and depth. I think your first
dozen or so casts are the most important because
this is often when you catch the largest bass. The
ones you catch at first are the most dominant fish.
Sometimes, you can keep a school "hot" as long as
you can keep a lure working through them, but
stopping for three or four minutes, or losing one
or two fish can turn off the entire school.

BASSMASTER: Overall, structure fishing really
involves a lot of trial and error, doesn't it?

DAVIS: Yes, it does. You're constantly learning as
you go. You really have to have the right mind-set
to keep casting and casting, and believe that eventually you're going to find the bass.

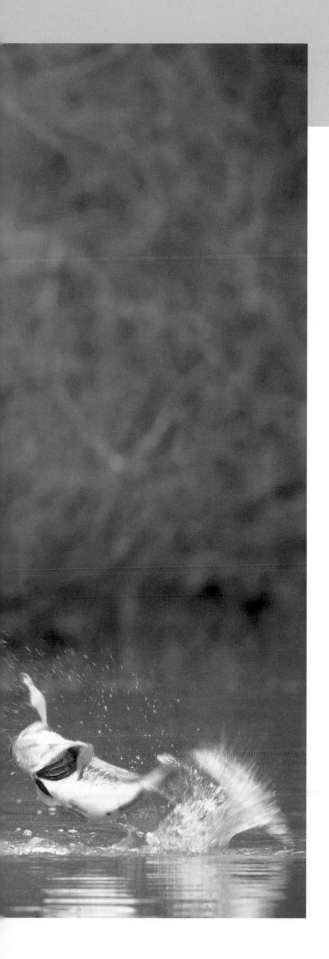

SEASONAL SITUATIONS

Cranking Through The
Four Seasons With Lipped Lures ...

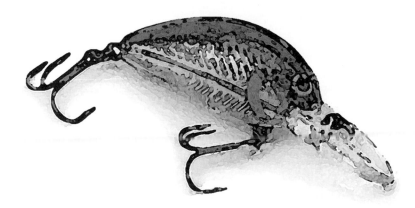

LOOK FOR a combination of structure and current when fishing crankbaits on rivers during the summer.

CRANKING FROM SUMMER TO FALL

Try these patterns and techniques for warm weather cranking

IT'S LATE SUMMER, a bright, steamy day without any promise of a breeze. The lake's surface is as shiny as a silver tray. The humidity and the temperature are both in the low 90s. This is when bass fishing is as much work as it is fun, especially if you're pulling crankbaits across a deep dropoff.

By midafternoon the two anglers are long past conversation. They simply stand in opposite ends of the boat, heaving long-billed baits as far as they can and then winding them back. Over and over. Cast and reel. Wipe away sweat. Swig Gatorade, and keep repeating the same motions.

It's a grueling effort, but not one that has gone without rewards. A large school of bass is feeding up and down this bar. At frequent intervals the anglers' baits have been the intended victims of murder. Now, a heavy load of would-be assassins sulk under the livewell's foamy spray.

Hot weather, cold weather. Fast retrieve, slow retrieve. Lots of smaller bass, a few giants. Crankbaits are among the most versatile of all lures, and they're highly effective in a broad range of fishing circumstances. They are truly lures for all seasons.

However, no single crankbait or crankbait technique is right for every season. Read on to find out how to be successful with crankbaits from summer into the autumn months.

(Opposite page) LOOK FOR bass holding near channel dropoffs, particularly on outside turns where current collides with the bend.

CRANKING THE RIVER

O.T. Fears is a pro angler from Oklahoma, recognized by his peers as a crankbait specialist, and he knows that summer is a banner time to use these baits.

He says several basic patterns are ideal for

FAT FREE FINGERLING

Crankbait Tip

Crankbaits are most effective when they contact bass holding structure. Their direction and unvarying mechanical action changes when the lure hits an object, giving the lure a much more realistic look to the bass. If you aren't bumping bottom or cover, slow down your retrieve until you are, or switch to a deeper crankbait.

BY EARLY summer, baitfish will have spawned and moved out to main channel areas. The bass will follow them, making offshore cranking a productive means of catching the roaming fish.

summer crankbaiting. Most of these apply to the mainstream section of a lake or river.

"By early summer, baitfish migrate from the coves and sloughs out to main channel areas, and the bass follow them there," Fears explains. "If there's current, the bass hold along structure where the flow carries the baitfish to them, and this is when crankbaits are really effective."

Fears' technique for fishing these spots is standard practice among river veterans. "I position my boat downstream and cast upstream past the spot. Then I pull my crankbait back with the flow. I try to bump the bait into the object and bring it around the side or over the object. When it squirts by the bass is when the fish will eat it."

One key to successful crankbaiting is to match lure size to the size of the forage. In early summer, young-of-year baitfish are small, so Fears casts a 1/4- or 3/8-ounce Norman Little N in shad and khaki/black colors. He says this and other baits with a wide side-to-side wobble are preferable during warm months.

CRANKING THE CURRENT

A second summer crankbait pattern is main lake areas of major reservoirs that have some current, however slight. "Basically, this is just like a river, except the territory's bigger, and you're usually fishing deeper," Fears continues.

In reservoirs, bass hang on or near channel dropoffs, particularly on outside turns where current washes up onto the bar. Fears says a combination of this condition plus a hump, point or some other "spot on the spot" will attract fish.

"I find these places with my depthfinder, and I position my boat downstream from them. Then I cast upstream and pull my bait back with the current. This is the natural direction for food to move to the fish."

Because he's usually working deeper spots than in rivers, Fears' choice of baits, tackle and cast/retrieve methods changes. "Now I'll go to a Norman DD-22. I want something that'll get down to 15 to 25 feet and dig the bottom and bang into the stumps. Also, I'll switch to a 7-foot medium action rod so I can cast farther. A long

MARK DAVIS' favorite fall hot spot is a shallow mud flat abutting a deep channel. He will position his boat over the channel, and cast upstream across the flat. Strikes occur as the bait hits the transition zone between shallow and deep water.

Going Lipless

An alternative to cranking deep cover in summertime and fall is to fish lipless crankbaits around schooling fish and in deep, standing timber.

"In some lakes, when the shad fry move out to the mainstream areas, bass school up to feed on them. Sometimes they'll be working below surface-feeding white bass, and other times they'll feed on the surface themselves. Surface-feeding is more likely to take place on calm mornings," says O.T. Fears.

He recommends a lipless crankbait for this condition, since they can be cast a long way, can be burned through the water to simulate terror-stricken shad, and have rattlers that attract bass by sound.

And then there are times when anglers can't see schooling bass. "They might school off a windy point or an island that's out next to the river channel. In places with a lot of milfoil or hydrilla, bass will school where the wind is blowing in on that area. You won't see

them, but they'll be there, and you can make a good catch if you can find them."

Fears does this by staying on the move, covering a lot of water in high percentage areas and random-casting with his vibrating bait. If he gets a strike, he continues casting back to the same spot until action subsides.

"Eighty or 90 percent of the time, they'll hit the bait on a straight, fast retrieve. But sometimes you have to use a little finesse with it. I've had times when I caught more bass with a stop-and-go retrieve, but pulling it up with my rod, then dropping the tip and letting the bait flutter down. I'd do this over and over pretty

fast, and almost every time they'd take it on the fall. You just have to experiment to see what the fish want."

Bass scattered in flooded timber is one more classic hot weather crankbait opportunity.

Fears continues, "For this situation, you need a bait that'll swim down to around 15 feet. You want to get it deep among the trees and bump the trunks. The bass will be suspended close to the trunks, usually on the shady side if the sun is bright."

Fears starts fishing timber on the submerged wood's outside edges. Then he turns in and works his way down creek channels, ditches or roadbeds that wind through the snags.

cast gives more distance to get the bait down into the strike zone."

A third productive summer crankbait pattern, especially in reservoirs with no current, is twitching a Rogue minnow plug parallel to boathouses and docks. "Almost every boathouse or floating dock has some sunken brushpiles around it. The bass will hold in these, or they'll get underneath the flotation, where it's shady. One of the deadliest techniques I know in the hottest part of the summer is working a Rogue alongside these places." Fears states.

His technique is simple. "Jerk the bait under the water to around 3 or 4 feet. Then use a stop-and-go action — reel it a couple of feet, stop and twitch it, then reel a little more. You want an erratic motion,

"This is a 'reaction' retrieve. The fish lying under the docks or around the brush see the bait, and they get excited and dart out and grab it." Fears says there are two basic lure colors for this technique: chrome with blue back for cloudy days, and chrome with black back for sunny days.

WHEN BASS ARE holding tight to cover in moving water, O.T. Fears cranks the lure so that it strikes a wooden object like a stump.

Tackle Selection With Davis

Regarding crankbait tackle, Mark Davis admits to being "kind of old-fashioned." He uses 6- and 6 1/2 foot

rods, and he prefers fiberglass because of its parabolic action, in which the rod flex is dispersed over more of the shaft.

"I do believe in limber rods with these baits," he says. For locations other than heavy timber, he prefers 10- to 14-pound-test line.

"Also, on clear lakes like Ouachita, I throw real small baits on spinning tackle rigged with 6- and 8-pound line. You need the line to get distance in a clear lake. It's critical to get the bait a long way out from the boat. Also, I can get the bait deeper on lighter line."

Davis says fall bass can be fickle in terms of retrieve speeds they will accept.

"One day they might want it fast, and the next they'll want it slow," he has found. "You just have to experiment to find the best speed."

CRANKING THE CREEKS

Veteran bass angler Mark Davis says fall is unquestionably a prime time for using the lipped lures. "When the water temperature starts dropping, baitfish swim back into the creeks and coves, and the bass follow them. Their main objective is to feed and get heavy for the cold of winter. They'll gorge themselves on shad, and they'll also eat crawfish along rocky areas."

Davis says his favorite fall hot spot is a mud flat toward the back of a creek or tributary that drops off into a creek channel. The top of the drop should be anywhere from 3 to 15 feet deep. "Those are places I find schools of bass, and I use crankbaits to locate them," he says

Davis' techniques for finding these fish are simple. "I just hold my boat over the channel and cast onto the flat and pull the bait over the dropoff. Or, if the fish are holding extremely tight to stumps or the lip of a drop, I'll fish the other direction, from deep to shallow. Crankbaits get more bottom contact coming up the drop," he says.

"Either way, I might fish a mile or more, starting at the middle of the bay and working back until I find bass.

"And here's something else about fishing those creeks," Davis continues. "Say you've got a few scattered stumps or logs, and they're submerged, so you can't see them. If you can find a piece of this structure, it's likely to have fish on it. I'll use a crankbait to find these spots. Now, the bass might not hit the bait, especially if it's right after a cold front. They'll be holding tight to cover, and they won't be very active. But after I find the stump, I can throw a jig in there several times in a row and probably catch that fish. So it takes both baits: The crankbait to find the structure, and the jig to work it."

CRANKING THE LAYDOWNS

Besides creek channels, Mark Davis also likes to work crankbaits along laydowns.

"Some crankbaits are better than others for fishing these logs," Davis explains. "Most people think you need a shallow running bait in 3 to 4 feet of water, but this isn't right. You're better off using a deep running bait. Because these baits have long bills, they don't hang up nearly as bad as shallow runners. You can bring one down a log or through a treetop a lot easier than you can with a short bill. One of my favorite baits to do this with is a Rebel Deep Mini-R."

Wobbling In The Creeks

In fall, Mark Davis likes crankbaits with a wide wobble. "The bass are active, and they want baits that behave the same way," he believes.

Regarding crankbait color, he says that when the water temperature drops below 50 degrees, he always tries a solid-red bait. "Don't ask me why they like red in cold water, but they do. This has been true everywhere I've fished in this situation."

Even more reliable is Davis' favorite fall crankbait pattern: "Overall, if I had to say just one thing about fishing a crankbait in the fall, it would be to find a creek to your liking, one that's got structure in it that you're sure holds a school of fish. Then, just tie on a bait that matches the water depth, put your trolling motor down and start moving along the channel drop and casting. It won't take very long to cover that whole area and find the bass. This is a very efficient technique for a great time to fish."

Davis says the proper way to fish laydowns is to parallel the trunks, scraping the bait along the bark. "You have to finesse the bait in the cover. I do it mostly by turning my reel. And this is one time I'll use extremely heavy line. I may go as high as 25-pound test. You don't need lighter line, since you're not making long casts, and the bait doesn't need to get down deep."

He says it's hard for anglers not accustomed to fishing crankbaits in heavy cover to work them through limbs. "You have to learn not to pull the bait into something so hard it'll hang up. Instead, you ease it through the cover, and when it bumps into something, relax the pressure and let it float up. But at the same time, you've got to be able to tell when the pressure is a fish. A lot of concentration is needed to fish this pattern, probably more than is needed for fishing a jig or a worm."

WINDY CRANKING

One final fall bassing pattern preferred by Davis is to bump crawfish-colored crankbaits along wind-exposed banks, points, pockets, riprap and other rocky spots. "That wave action moves the crawfish around, and bass move into that extremely shallow water looking for them," he says. "This is true on most all lakes. I'm talking about spots where there's a mudline, where the wind's really got the bank churned up."

CRANKY BRONZEBACKS

Caution: Crankbait fishing for smallmouth can lead to violence

SMASHED IT!" "Delivered a crushing blow!" "Almost ripped my arm from its socket!"

These comments are not from participants in a professional wrestling match, but from anglers reliving the experience of cranking up smallmouth. Unlike the occasional lackadaisical hit from a large-mouth bass, when smallmouth attack a crankbait, it's always a no-holds-barred encounter. And if you're not careful, someone is going to get hurt.

BEST BAIT

"Twenty years ago, a crankbait would not have been my first choice for smallmouth bass, but that has changed," says Jeff Snyder, a professional angler and smallmouth expert who frequents the lakes and rivers of the Midwest. "Today, the crankbait is my bread-and-butter lure for quickly locating aggressive smallmouth. Nothing else triggers as hard a strike."

In the Northwest, Washington state tournament

angler Bill Roberts readily admits smallmouth are his favorite fish, and crankbaits are his No. 1 presentations.

"Smallmouth have an attitude toward crankbaits that largemouth sometimes lack," he acknowledges.

"Crankbaits are versatile because they can represent both crawfish and baitfish," continues Roberts. "It depends on the time of year and the particular water you are fishing as to whether smallies are feeding on crawfish or some type of minnow. However, I use the same crankbaits to imitate both prey by selecting models that have good action and different depth ranges. My bait preferences include Worden's Timber Tiger series and Poe's Competition series."

Snyder believes vibration is critically important in choosing a crankbait. "For smallmouth, more so than largemouth, I want a crankbait that has a tight wiggle rather than a loose wobble, and one that can be retrieved at high speeds. But that's not to say a crankbait should always be fished by winding rapidly. A good crankbait must be equally effective at all retrieve speeds. And it should be available in several depth models to strain the water. That's why I like the Bandit series, ranging from the supershallow Footloose to the No. 300."

SEASONAL SECRETS

Roberts loves to crank the waters of the Northwest, including California's Lake Shasta, Washington's Banks Lake and the Columbia River.

"There are some anglers who try to tell me that smallmouth can't be taken on crankbaits in water temperatures less than 50 degrees or over 70 degrees. That just isn't so," states Roberts. "Heck, I've caught smallies on crankbaits in 42 degree water, and those fish wanted it bad — almost ripping the rod out of my hand. And I've taken smallies on crankbaits during the hottest days of summer — as long as I could reach them with the bait.

"One of the worst things anglers can do is get stuck in a false belief about 'magic' temperatures."

Snyder, who cranks for smallmouth any time the surface isn't covered with ice, agrees whole-

USE A CRANKBAIT with a tight wiggle for catching smallmouth in cooling water.

heartedly with Roberts. "Fish cannot escape their environment," he says. "Yes, you must be aware that in cooler water, a bass' metabolism will be slower. But the metabolism affects how fish digest food and how often they need to feed. That does not mean they are necessarily slower in attacking a lure that is moving.

"I do not pay that much attention to temperature anymore because I've become a firm believer that when prey and predator meet, the potential of a strike is there — regardless of the temperature. Crankbaits can draw strikes any time of the season — you just have to adjust your presentation to find the right retrieve."

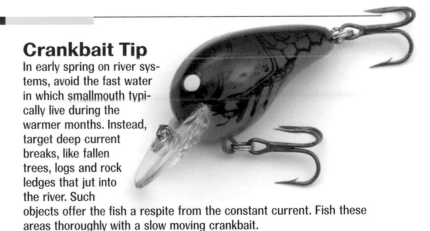

Crankbait Tip
In early spring on river systems, avoid the fast water in which smallmouth typically live during the warmer months. Instead, target deep current breaks, like fallen trees, logs and rock ledges that jut into the river. Such objects offer the fish a respite from the constant current. Fish these areas thoroughly with a slow moving crankbait.

River Cranking

When it comes to jockeying for feeding positions, smallmouth use current to their advantage. Because smallmouth are creatures of current, Jeff Snyder seldom considers using a crankbait in a lake situation unless the wind is blowing. But in flowing water, it's a different case.

"Crankbaits are my primary tools for rivers or any waterway connections with current," states Snyder. "With a single bait, such as a Bandit 200, I can cover 80 percent of a typical river's smallmouth habitat. By holding the rod tip at various positions, I can strain the depths to 8 feet. And by reeling fast or slow, I can vary the speed of retrieve until I figure out what the bass want on that particular day."

When fishing for largemouth with a crankbait, Snyder wants to bump bottom objects. But when cranking for smallmouth, he says a free swimming retrieve is every bit as effective. This is particularly important when fishing rocky bottom cover in a strong current. There is no need to use deep diving baits to overdive, thereby sacrificing lures to rocks. A crankbait that dives close to the bottom — only brushing the bottom occasionally — is sufficient.

Snyder explains that while smallmouth in impoundments move deeper in the summer, river smallmouth actually move shallower — into faster moving water.

On small to moderate-size rivers during the warmwater period, Snyder heads first to the "pushes," where the water rises at the heads of riffles. In the shallowest water, he goes to a Bandit Foot-Loose, which runs less than 1 foot under the surface. He also favors current seams and reverse flow eddies along wing dams, riprap, bridge piers and inflowing tributaries. Snyder recommends fishing a crankbait past any object that breaks the current flow.

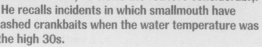

With the arrival of cold water in the late fall, smallmouth move out of the stronger current flow sites to slower eddies or holes. While Snyder still relies on a crankbait as his initial search lure, he slows the retrieve considerably.

He recalls incidents in which smallmouth have smashed crankbaits when the water temperature was in the high 30s.

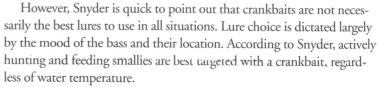

However, Snyder is quick to point out that crankbaits are not necessarily the best lures to use in all situations. Lure choice is dictated largely by the mood of the bass and their location. According to Snyder, actively hunting and feeding smallies are best targeted with a crankbait, regardless of water temperature.

Also, he prefers cranking when smallmouth are shallower than 8 feet, and he never employs crankbaits if bass are deeper than 12 feet.

"But the single most important factor for crankbait use is water movement," continues Snyder. "On a lake, a breeze or wind must be blowing; on a reservoir, the dam must be pulling water. Of course, in a river, the steady current opens the possibility of cranking for smallmouth every day."

SEASONAL BREAKDOWN

• *Spring Patterns* — Roberts believes cool water in lakes during the early spring is the cranker's best friend. His reasoning is simple: Smallmouth are on the move from deeper wintering areas to the shallower flats. This requires anglers to search considerable stretches of water, making crankbait use ideal for this situation. And because few anglers in his region attempt cranking at this time, it remains an almost untapped gold mine for those who do.

"Most of my early spring and prespawn cranking is along those migration routes, such as rocky points, creek channels leading into bays, or shallow flats. Transition areas where soft muck bottom switches to rock rubble or a firmer bottom also are key sites. Key fishing depths are 7 to 14 feet."

But according to Roberts, the real secret to coldwater cranking is "hanging" the bait. Each time he bumps a bottom object, he pauses the retrieve to allow the bait to hang in the water. Roberts achieves neutral buoyancy by using Storm's SuspenDots. For his favorite Poe's 300, he says six dots positioned directly on top of one another, immediately in front of the first treble, usually does the trick. However, because these wood baits are not identical in weight, some adjustment in the number of adhesive 'Dots may be needed.

How important is a suspending crankbait in cold water? Roberts tells about a Banks Lakes tournament one spring when he had a limit in eight minutes with one of his doctored baits and a stalling retrieve. Meanwhile, his boat partner — using an unweighted crankbait — didn't catch a single bass during the flurry.

Once smallmouth arrive on the shallow flats, the Timber Tiger DC-8 becomes Roberts' mainstay. With water temperature well into the 50s and the bass holding in water less than 8 feet deep, he says

THE STEADY current in a river system provides the setting for daylong cranking.

there is no need to use suspending baits. "Now I'm using a steady retrieve, moving the bait a bit faster," notes Roberts. "With its Timber Roller Lip, the DC-8 has very good deflecting capability for both rock and wood, along with that perfect tight wiggling action."

• *Summer Patterns* — With the spawn over and the shallows heating up, smallmouth in lakes drop deeper. Roberts makes the adjustment by going to a Poe's 400 Competition to reach the 14- to 16-foot depths, or Poe's Long Reach to hit the 18- to 20-foot range. He targets extended points, rockpiles on deep flats, midlake humps, and ledges along river channels.

"I'll start the morning off by cranking fast in order to cover a lot of water during the low light period," explains Roberts. "Then as the day wears on, I slow down and work the crankbait more methodically. By this, I mean picking apart those larger structural elements and isolating individual pieces of submerged cover, such as stumps or large rocks. I want to hit something, then pause to let the crankbait back off and begin floating upward before engaging it again."

This bump-and-back-off technique replaces his bump-and-hover tactic of spring.

• *Fall Patterns* — When the lake begins to cool off in the fall, and smallmouth return to shallower water, these experts agree that nothing can put bass in the boat as quickly as a crankbait.

Roberts says his retrieves in the fall are markedly different than those in spring or summer. "Using one of the Timber Tiger models, I simply wind the reel handle as fast as I can — I literally burn the bait," he explains. "Timber Tigers, particularly the DC-5, hold a straight line while maintaining that crankbait action, no matter how quickly they are retrieved. That's how I get my largest smallmouth of the fall."

SMALLMOUTH experts use crankbaits in water shallower than 8 feet but not deeper than 12 feet.

FISH SUBMERGED WEEDBEDS with a shallow crank that cruises above the grass.

CRANKING IN THE GRASS

One of bass fishing's top performers reveals an obscure bass-catching technique

OIL AND WATER. Cats and dogs. French food and hot sauce. Some things simply aren't made to go together.

What about crankbaits and aquatic grass? No way, you say? Think these baits would stay too glommed up in the greenery to draw strikes from bass?

"This pattern can be awesome. I mean, it can absolutely be the best thing you've ever tried," affirms Kevin VanDam. "When conditions are right, no other bait or fishing method can come close to it for locating and catching bass in grassbeds."

So, following are details of this unique technique refined by its innovator. First, a warning: It isn't easy to duplicate. It calls for specialized tackle. It requires considerable practice to master, and intense concentration to employ successfully. Nevertheless, anglers who follow VanDam's instructions to the letter will be rewarded with hefty catches of grassbed bass, even on days when other methods and spots strike out.

THE SYSTEM

Many lakes around the United States are infested with milfoil, hydrilla and other aquatic grasses. Where this vegetation exists, bass gravitate to it like toddlers to an ice cream truck. When grass grows in a lake, there is no better cover to try.

However, grassbeds can be difficult to fish. Some span many acres, and bass can be hard to pinpoint. They tend to concentrate in small, specific areas — true "needles in a haystack." Thus, anglers need a method that enables them to cover a lot of water while quickly eliminating unproductive zones.

This is what VanDam accomplishes by fishing

(Opposite page) KEVIN VANDAM positions his boat over the deep edge of a grassline and follows its path while casting a crankbait.

Crankbait Tip

What do bass see in clear crankbaits? Very little. Therein lies the secret to their success in clear water. These lures have the same action, emit the same sonic pulsations and bounce and grind through cover in the same fashion as painted versions. But their transparency shows bass a muted, ghostly apparition of a baitfish that can be deadly.

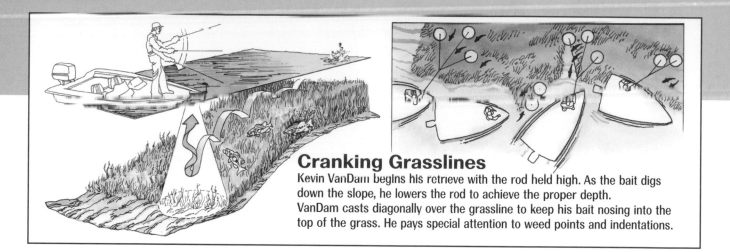

Cranking Grasslines

Kevin VanDam begins his retrieve with the rod held high. As the bait digs down the slope, he lowers the rod to achieve the proper depth. VanDam casts diagonally over the grassline to keep his bait nosing into the top of the grass. He pays special attention to weed points and indentations.

crankbaits in grass — or, more specifically, along grass edges.

"I can cover five times more water with this technique than I can with a plastic worm or a jig, and I can keep my bait in the strike zone all the time," he says. "Also, this system gives me a means for finding points or cuts in the grass where bass are most likely to hold."

VanDam says this pattern is best from June through September. After bass spawn, they migrate back to deep grasslines, where they linger until the water temperature starts dropping again in fall. They feed along the edges of the cover. When they're not feeding, they sink down in it.

He prefers to fish weedlines with edges that angle down rather than drop vertically. He says milfoil beds typically do this, whereas hydrilla tends to grow off the bottom in a straight wall.

"I use a depthfinder to position my boat over the deep edge of a grassline, then I follow it wherever it goes," he explains. "I hold over the last few sprigs of grass growing up next to open water.

"Then, if the grass edge angles down, I cast diagonally across it and work my bait back shallow to deep. If the grass grows vertically, I cast parallel to it — but this situation is far less productive than a sloping grassline. I always fish a tapered, irregular edge if I can find one."

When running this pattern, anglers must be acutely aware of the depth of the cover and the bottom and how deep their lure will dive. VanDam says a typical scenario is for a milfoil bed to be 3 feet below the surface on the shallow side, then angle down to 9 feet at the bottom edge.

"I'll troll along that 9-foot junction of grass and open water. The bass will be somewhere along the

slope, either barely above the grass or down in it. In either case, they're in a good position to grab my crankbait when it swims by," he believes.

THE TACKLE

Using the right tackle is critical in VanDam's method for fishing crankbaits in grass.

"This presentation requires a rod with plenty of sensitivity," he says. "I use a Quantum Tour Edition 7-foot graphite popping/crankbait rod. This one piece rod has a medium-light action that's perfect for feeling a crankbait as it digs into the grass.

"I match this with a Quantum Pro 1C baitcasting reel, which has a 5:1 gear ratio. I don't like a high speed reel for this technique. I spool up with Berkley Trilene XT green line. This line is very abrasion resistant, and this is important when you're popping a crankbait through grass all day."

In lures, VanDam typically fishes a Model 7A Bomber in a variety of colors. Sometimes he prefers a larger 8A Bomber if he is keying specifically on big bass. Also, he says a Storm Wiggle Wart is good with this technique. "You need a crankbait with a wide-wobbling action," he advises. He attaches his bait to his line with a snap to allow freer movement and to facilitate quick bait changes when he needs to try different colors.

When crankbaiting in grass, VanDam rigs four identical rods and baits. The only difference is line size. He explains, "The diameter of the line controls the diving depth of the lure. So, I'll rig one rod with 10-pound test, one with 12-pound, one with 14-pound, and one with 17-pound. Then, I use whatever combination matches the water depth under the boat."

If I'm running a grassline that's 9 feet deep along the outside edge, I'll use the rod with the

10-pound-test line. This way, I know I'm using tackle that'll keep my bait in the cover all the way back to the boat," he reveals.

THE METHOD

Positioning the boat and using the right tackle and lures are the first steps. Next comes the actual fishing process.

"I cast diagonally up the sloping grassline," VanDam instructs. "I don't make long casts. The average length is probably 20 yards."

When he starts his retrieve, VanDam holds his rod high, and he reels the crankbait down until it hits grass. "This is where the sensitive rod tip is so important. You have to be able to feel what the lure's doing," he advises. "When the wiggle stops and I feel pressure, I quit reeling and hold tension on the lure for a second or two. If there's no movement, I assume the bait's in the grass. I drop my rod tip for a couple more seconds to allow the bait to begin floating up, and I pop the rod with my wrists to jerk the lure free of the grass. Then I continue reeling until the bait hits the next piece of grass, and I repeat this process.

"I do this over and over, maybe five to 10 times per cast. The bait 'bumps' into the grass. I pause it, then pop it free and reel it a couple more yards until it snugs in the grass again. Also, I hold my rod tip progressively lower as I reel the bait deeper along the grass edge. When the bait is close to the boat, my rod is almost pointed down toward it."

VanDam describes this basic retrieve as "worming a crankbait," because the lure traces a path that's similar to the lift-and-drop action of a plastic worm. He never intends for his bait to penetrate into the grass more than a foot.

VanDam says it is imperative to keep the crankbait free of grass.

"If you're dragging grass, the cast is wasted. A bass won't hit the lure," he notes. "However, by allowing the bait to float up a couple of seconds, then snapping the rod with your wrists, the bait will clean itself of grass almost every time. I'd say out of 100 casts, I have 95 where I work the bait back to the boat without trailing any grass.

"One other important tip: Most strikes come when you pop the lure," VanDam stresses. "Bass follow the bait, or they lie down in the grass watching it, and when they see that fast little deflection, they strike reflexively."

Running The Pattern

To pattern crankbait bass in the grass, Kevin VanDam searches for irregularities in the cover where bass are most likely to hold: points of grass, cuts, thicker clumps or anything else different from a straight, grassy edge.

"I find these places with my lure," VanDam states. "Say I'm working along a grassline, and I've figured out the angle to keep my bait working down the taper and barely penetrating the grass. But then I make a cast, and the bait really digs into the grass, or it misses the grass totally. I know something has changed on that grassline, and I'll adjust my next casts in or out to relocate the edge.

"This is typically a point or a cut, and it's a high percentage spot. I'll usually pick up a few bass scattered randomly along a grassline, but these irregular places are where they really gang up."

VanDam says bass are very consistent in how they relate to grasslines from day to day. "One day they may hold near the shallow side of the break; the next day, they're close to the deep edge," he says. "But once you learn the pattern — which includes their depth and whether they're up chasing bait or burrowed into the grass — then you can go from spot to spot and find them in the same places. Because you know where your bait is, it's easy to duplicate this pattern."

One other note: When VanDam locates a concentration of bass, and after he works the spot thoroughly with his crankbait, he will do likewise with a plastic worm or jig. "Sometimes I can pick up another couple of fish with this slower bait. It doesn't take long to try, and it's definitely worth the effort."

NO OTHER LURE can effectively intercept migrating prespawn bass better than a crankbait.

PRESPAWN CRANKING
You may think it's still too cold for diving plugs, but it's not

THE CALENDAR READ late March, but the slicing wind that blew across northern Indiana's Barbee Chain of Lakes felt more like January. And if the bone-chilling temperatures weren't enough of a reminder that ol' man winter hadn't surrendered to spring, that morning's light snowfall was.

That didn't keep Bassmaster Roger Miller and other Hoosier anglers from searching for bass that prowl the weed edges shortly after the ice leaves Indiana lakes. But, as most of the fishermen probed with dainty tube baits, grubs and jigs, Miller machine-gunned the flats and shallow ledges with crankbaits.

"The average fisherman probably thinks I'm nuts for fishing crankbaits shallow this early in the year," says the avid crankbaiter. "But there's not a better way to find active prespawn bass than with a crankbait."

Miller proved that point by catching several bass,

then emphasized it when a dazed 5-pound largemouth, with a Shad Rap clenched inside its jaws, rolled onto the surface. There were no jumps or long runs, but from the way the bait was buried deep inside the fish's mouth, it was obvious that this sluggish bass had no trouble catching up with the crankbait in cold water. That dispelled yet another myth about prespawn bass, says Miller.

"A bass may not chase a crankbait for a great distance, but bang one around its head and it will go for it," he adds.

ULTIMATE SEARCH WEAPON

Don't think that only Yankee bass are dumb enough to hit crankbaits in early spring, either. Examine the lures and techniques that dominate prespawn tournaments and you'll realize that crankbaits — shallow divers, deep divers and the lipless variety — are deadly when bass are staging on structure between wintering holes and spawning flats.

Crankbait king David Fritts believes crankbaits have an edge over other lures when the bass are sluggish.

"The crankbait triggers reflex strikes by doing things that worms or jigs can't do," says Fritts. "For example, when one of those spring cold fronts passes, and the bass shut off, you can get them to strike a crankbait by banging it off rocks, stumps or the bottom."

Without question, jigs, jerkbaits and spinnerbaits will catch prespawn bass, too. But when bass are moving on structure and might be anywhere between deep and shallow water, no other lure covers the water faster, as effectively or as thoroughly, says fellow crankbait aficionado Mark Davis.

"It's my choice for finding bass that I may catch better on other lures," says the Arkansas pro. "I use the crankbait as a search tool, and once I locate the bass, I'll experiment with other lures to find out which ones they want best. Many times, the crankbait remains the best of them all."

PRESPAWN WARMUP

And another thing: Warming water triggers bass movements to staging areas, but the "magic" temperature varies from one end of the country to the other.

For example, pro Gerald Beck says North Carolina bass often begin to stage with the arrival of the first warming trend, and crankbait fishing gets hot when the water temperature reaches the mid-50s. But it happens at lower temperatures in the North, says Michigan's Kevin VanDam.

"I've caught limits of bass that averaged more than 5 pounds from lakes that had been covered with ice a few days before," says VanDam. "Northern bass are accustomed to cold water, so they are more active in lower temperatures. Anglers who think they've got to fish deep for early prespawn bass are missing out on some of the finest fishing of the season."

Especially if that lake is shallow and has a stained or dark color, adds Miller.

Crankbait Tip

In late winter and early spring, search out sunlit shorelines during warming trends. In particular, focus on rocky shorelines, bluffs and riprap where these rock formations conduct heat and warm the surrounding water. Work the bait parallel to these areas, using a slow, steady retrieve. Remember, the water is warmer but the fish are still sluggish.

Crankbait Secrets

Try these tricks to enjoy more crankbait action on preopawn bass.

■ Work into the wind to maintain boat control along offshore weedlines. Toss a marker buoy overboard to mark a spot in case you're blown off the spot while playing a fish.

■ For largemouth, use lures with bright colors and rattles in dark water, and dark or natural-colored lures in clear water. Smallmouth tend to like noisy, bright-colored crankbaits under all conditions.

■ Experiment with line sizes. Most natural lake crankers use 10- and 12-pound-test line. However, if you want a lure to run deeper, use smaller line and make longer casts. Conversely, if a lure runs too deep, try heavier line and make shorter casts.

■ Use a split ring or a snap. Lures perform better with them. Snaps make it easier to change lures, but they need to be checked frequently to make sure they haven't come undone.

■ Probe dropoffs at channel mouths that connect two lakes. Boat traffic actually improves crankbait fishing, so it's a good pattern for midday summer fishing.

■ Crank over the heads of smallmouth. Largemouth prefer a bait near the bottom, but smallmouth like to come up for the bait.

■ Keep hooks sharp and replace them when needed. Treble hooks weaken after extended use.

■ Mark your lucky crankbaits. If a crankbait catches fish, mark the bill with a waterproof marker so you don't confuse it with unproven lures of the same color and model. Inexplicably, some lures seem to have more bass appeal than others of the same make and model.

"One day when much of the Barbee Chain was still covered with ice, I caught 25 bass at lunchtime on Shad Raps," he says. "The water temperature was only 36 degrees."

Terry says mid-50 degree water is the key temperature for mid-South cranking, but Deep South bass require warmer temperatures. Regardless of where you fish, he adds, prespawn bass are highly susceptible to the crankbait.

"It's been my experience that early prespawn fish don't go for a jig or worm as well as they do a crankbait," he explains. "Once the water temp begins to rise and they're starting to think about the spawn, they seem to automatically react to moving lures like crankbaits."

CRANKING SPOTS

Crankbaits are effective during prespawn periods on a variety of waters, ranging from shallow, weedy lakes to highland reservoirs. As a rule, though, shallower lakes are better for prespawn cranking than deep waters because the bass are more likely to stage in water depths that are accessible to most crankbaits.

Even so, Beck prefers to find prespawn bass in water ranging from 12 to 15 feet and on main lake points outside the spawning areas. He says bass will really school up on points leading into major coves.

"I prefer fishing that depth because that's where the big females seem to congregate," he explains. "Once they leave deep water, they scatter. If you can find where they hold on those deep points before the spawn, you can count on a couple of weeks of fabulous crankbait fishing."

Similarly, bass in northern natural lakes stage on main lake points or in a weedline growing along a dropoff. If the water is stained, you can find them gathering in 5 to 12 feet of water.

"The weed growth will dictate the depth where you should concentrate that time of year," says VanDam. "Once you determine the depth at which the weeds stop growing, that's as deep as you need to fish."

That strategy applies to reservoirs with grass, too. Storm Lures' Jim Morton says hydrilla beds adjacent to spawning areas can hold a tremendous school of prespawn bass.

"I start looking for them in the 10- to 14-foot depths between deeper water and a bedding area," explains Morton, also a veteran tournament angler. "If there's grass there, they will relate to the grasslines."

Many staging areas can be found by simply identifying the spawning grounds, then scrutinizing the immediate area to determine the route the bass use to move from deep to shallow. Points are the most obvious routes of travel, but finding where on the point the bass will stage isn't easy. That's why Fritts looks for rocks on those points or along creek ledges.

"I really like a crawfish crankbait that time of year," he says. "It seems that early bass are feeding on crawfish, so rocks are the likely place for them to hang out."

Once you find a likely staging spot, don't give up on it, adds Beck. He cranks potential hot spots several times.

Beyond The Obvious

Kansas pro Cecil Kingsley is an expert at honing in on prespawn bass on the highland reservoirs of the Missouri Ozarks. To find fish in these popular impoundments, Kingsley starts on the first point of a cove, and he test-fishes his way back into the cove.

"Now, when I say that I cover a lot of water in a hurry, I mean that I fish here for a little while and there for a little while, to hunt and peck for 'em. But I don't hurry when it comes to lure speed. Retrieves must be very slow. You always keep that bait coming at a crawl. It's almost like slow rolling a spinnerbait. If you get too fast with it, they won't hit it."

When searching for prespawn bass, Kingsley concentrates on stretches of bank that are different from the norm.

"Banks that are close to deep water are best," he says. "Everybody knows that. But I also look for less obvious differences, things like underwater weedlines or mudlines, a rock dropoff, a short rock bank flanked by mud or clay. These places are an awful lot better than, say, a rock bank that runs for a long way. An underwater stumpfield is good, or a tree that's a different type from all the others around it. You just need to be observant and try to go to something that's different from its surroundings."

CRANKBAITS trigger reflex strikes from coldwater bass, the experts say.

"If you have a pretty good idea where the bass stage before they move into the spawning areas, check it often," he explains. "You can fish a spot several times during the day without catching a fish, and on that fifth time, load the boat."

The weather plays a role in where or how you're going to catch prespawn bass on crankbaits. Most pros believe that the wind

blowing onto a potential staging area makes it even better for crankbait fishing.

"If the bass have been suspended off the banks and you get a windy day, that will draw the fish to the structure and get them feeding," explains Davis. "When I see wind forecast during the prespawn season, I feel certain I can catch them on a crankbait."

And if you're a deep water cranker, adds Beck, cloudy days are a nemesis. Sunshine helps hold the bass on the structure or near the cover, where they are easier to target. On cloudy days, the fish tend to roam more.

TIGHT WIGGLING crankbaits produce when bass are feeding on baitfish. A wide wobbling crankbait is the choice when the bass are feeding on crawfish.

CRANKBAIT STRATEGIES

Even the pros don't agree on which type of crankbaits — wide wobblers like Morton's Storm Wiggle Wart, or tight wigglers like Terry's Shad Rap — are best-suited for the early season.

A lot depends upon what the fish are eating, says former biologist fishing pro Ken Cook.

"If the fish are keying on baitfish, especially in clear water, then the tighter wiggle may be better," he explains. "But if they're feeding on crawfish or the water is heavily stained, then the wide wobble is better because it produces more vibration."

Lure speed becomes a factor, too. You need to slow down to keep the lure in the fish's face longer, but don't do so at the expense of losing action or deflection qualities. An effective prespawn crankbait makes unexpected moves while banging off the cover.

That works in vegetation, too, explains Miller. One of his favorite techniques is to crank Shad Raps into weed patches and "rip" them out. The bait jumping out of the weeds, plus the hesitation that follows, often triggers violent strikes.

"It's a lot of work because your lure often clogs in the weeds and the cast is wasted," he explains. "But if there are bass in those weeds and you can stay with it, you're going to catch fish."

Davis prefers to throw small baits on light line and spinning tackle in the early season, especially in clear water. The reason? To make longer casts and get the lure to run deeper.

"If a guy can put a small crankbait in 10 feet of water where everyone else is throwing a big crankbait, he's going to catch more fish," says Davis.

Line size also is an important consideration when fishing lipless crankbaits during the prespawn season. Lures like the Rat-L-Trap, Cordell Spot and Strike King Diamondback Shad are excellent for triggering reaction strikes from bass in the final stages of the prespawn period.

SUNNY DAYS are best for prespawn cranking because the bright light makes the fish hold nearer the cover, making target casting easier.

Early Season Cranking

Perhaps the most overlooked crankbait pattern is the one that begins early — like when the ice vanishes from the surface of a northern lake. Although the prespawn period is weeks away, bass staging off spawning flats move shallow during stable weather conditions.

Michigan pro Kevin VanDam agrees with this premise. When the water is less than 50 degrees, he prefers to crank Rebel Wee Rs and Model 7A Bombers at slow or medium speeds along the 5- to 10-foot dropoffs.

"Bass will slam a crankbait, but the lure must be presented closer to the fish because they won't travel a long way to strike," he explains. "The fish are usually concentrated on the classic structure, so those areas must be fished thoroughly."

Classic structure includes points and inside turns of holes and main lake dropoffs. The better areas offer weeds or rock. He works several depths, trying to zero in on the specific depth the fish are using. He casts parallel to the

break, making several casts within each depth zone.

TECHNIQUES FOR CRANKING

Apply These Methods

When All Else Fails …

CAROLINA RIGGING WITH CRANKBAITS

This unusual technique is extremely effective at catching those in-between bass of spring and summer

IT'S AN AGE-OLD PROBLEM in bass fishing — how to reach inactive bass that are suspended well below the surface and coax them into biting.

Bass enthusiasts have wrestled with this puzzling situation practically since boats first floated.

Chad Potts believes he has found a reliable solution, particularly when this dilemma presents itself in the warmer months. He refers to his trick as the "Suspend Rig."

"We developed this technique because suspended fish are just so hard to catch during the late spring and summer months," said Potts, an avid tournament angler from Fort Worth, Texas. "In my part of the country, the weather gets so hot that the fish suspend a lot of the time. We figured if we're going to do well in tournaments during this time, we were going to have to figure out a way to catch those suspended fish.

"I don't know of anybody else who's doing what we've been doing. I've heard of people Carolina rigging crankbaits, but they always use the typical 1-ounce weight and let it go all the way to the bottom, and let the crankbait suspend a foot or two off the bottom. Our technique is a lot different."

The answer to hot weather suspended bass is a hybrid form of Carolina rigging with diving plugs, a technique Potts and partner Jerry David of Pilot Park exploited to win more than $40,000 in two years of fishing local tournaments. It has produced handsomely on several Texas lakes, including Texoma, Whitney, Ray Roberts and Squaw Creek.

He explains why this tactic works so well.

"Big, deep diving crankbaits aren't the answer with these suspended fish, because the baits blow through the schools," Potts theorizes. "And if the bass are below 20 feet, you can't really reach them with a crankbait anyway.

"The key is being able to get a crankbait to stop at a certain level. Playing with

(Opposite page) FISHING A CRANKBAIT on a Carolina rig keeps the bait in the strike zone long enough to fool a bass into hitting the oddity.

Crankbait Tip

Store crankbaits inside plastic tackle system storage boxes, according to their running depth. Mark the depth range on the side of the box for easy reference. You will then have instant access to the organized baits based on the depth situation you encounter.

Refining A Crankbait Bite

In his heralded rookie BASS season, Tim Horton did the unthinkable. Not only did he win the coveted BASS Angler-of-the-Year award for 1999-2000 in his freshman year, but he did it in convincing fashion.

In the third event of the season, held on the Potomac River, Horton wrote the story of someone who understood how to find fish and then how to make them eat a crankbait.

Like so many great things, Horton's discovery of the 25- by 75-yard piece of structure that paved the way to victory started with a small but important observation. Having seen birds feeding on baitfish in the bay, Horton knew that something significant had to be holding that forage. And, if there was bait, there would certainly be bass.

Through a patient and careful search with his electronics, Horton eventually found a structure bedecked with several rocks that came to within 3 feet of the surface.

"Even with fish stacked on that spot, if I didn't make contact with those rocks, I couldn't get them to bite. But, through trial and error, I figured out that if I let the Cordell Spot get down in those rocks and pop it free, that was the deal," observes Horton.

"When you're on a spot like that one, you have the opportunity to really fine-tune your presentations. You can absolutely figure out what makes them bite and what doesn't."

Not only did Horton carefully hone his drop-and-pop presentation, he recognized that certain casting angles also produced more consistent responses.

In other fishing situations, notes Horton, the reasons for downturns in the action are not nearly as obvious. Still, a fisherman has to constantly re-evaluate the situation: If you've found fish, the best choice may be to simply stick it out and try to expand your area, try to find out if the fish have moved, and then try to catch them there.

In this tournament, he did both. Knowing that he had the fish to win, Horton didn't stray far, sensing that the bass had momentarily pulled off the rocks to the guts on either side. While he never caught a fish in these troughs, it wasn't for a lack of effort. In fact, as he ultimately proved, refining a crankbait bite requires equal parts observation and commitment.

---

this rig in a swimming pool, we found that we could use a Carolina rig to get a small crankbait as deep as we wanted it and use the buoyancy of the bait to stay at a certain level."

This form of Carolina rigging diving plugs begins with the proper tackle.

THE RIG

Potts utilizes a 6 1/2-foot medium/heavy action Piranha rod and a baitcasting reel. His 2- to 3-foot leader is made of 10- to 15-pound-test Berkley Big Game line. More important is the combination of split shot and small bullet weights he uses to precisely balance the rig so the crankbait floats well off the bottom and remains

relatively stationary at a certain level. Positioned below the weight, the split shot keeps the sinker out in front of the lure. With this tactic, you can either utilize a swivel to create a separate leader or simply use the main line.

Unlike most other attempts that combine Carolina rigging and crankbaits, this technique uses mostly shallow diving baits to approach schools of suspended bass in 15 to 35 feet of water.

"I like a shallow running bait because you don't have to put a bunch of weight on it to get it down," Potts says. "And the smaller crankbaits just seem to work better in these schools. That may be because bass down deep never see any small profile crankbaits. If they do see a crankbait, it's a big one. So the smaller ones give the fish a different look."

The small shallow divers that work best in this setup include Mann's Baby 1-Minus, Excalibur's Swim'N Image and Bomber's Fat Free Fingerling and Model A.

WHILE SOME anglers use deep diving crankbaits for Carolina rigging, Chad Potts uses shallow runners because they give the fish a different look.

Potts recommends the following weight/split shot combinations to achieve the appropriate descent rates:

- *Baby 1-Minus* — 1/16-ounce bullet weight and one split shot equals a fall rate of about 1 foot per 2 1/2 seconds; 1/8-ounce weight and four split shot, 1 foot per second.
- *Swim'N Image* — 1/16-ounce weight and one split shot, 1 foot per 2 seconds.
- *Fat Free Fingerling* — 1/16-ounce weight and one split shot, 1 foot every 2 seconds.
- *Model A* — 1/8-ounce weight with no split shot, 1 foot per second.

Fishermen should experiment with the weight to better match the water conditions on each particular day, according to Potts.

Although the action can sometimes be fast and furious when a well-balanced crankbait reaches a school of bass with this method, it is usually a painstakingly slow technique.

"There's really nothing to the retrieve. Sometimes we just free-line it and let the wind carry us, which is like making a long cast. We'll bump it a time or two, and it will take 10 or 15 minutes before you reel it in. It takes a lot of patience to work this technique."

THE TECHNIQUE

Basically, Potts makes a long cast and free-spools the reel to get extra distance. Then he counts the bait down as it sinks, typically at a rate of about a foot every 2 or 2 1/2 seconds (depending on the lure and weight). After reaching the desired (and approximate) depth level, he pops the rod upward slightly to make the crankbait hop erratically, then counts the lure back down.

"The key to making this technique work is being able to use your electronics," Potts emphasizes. "You have to be able to figure out the depth level of the schools and then be able to stay at the right level. If you're marking fish in 60 feet of water and 30 feet off the bottom, 30 feet is where your crankbait needs to be.

"Other than this technique, there's no other

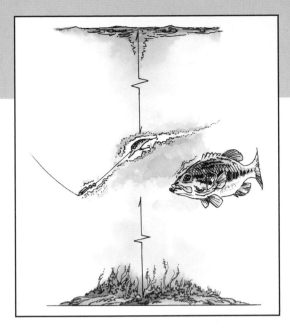

THE KEY to catching suspended bass on a Carolina rigged crankbait is to count the rig down to the most productive depth.

real way to do that. You can't really drop a worm down and stop it at 30 feet. But by using your depthfinder, with this method, you can really make pinpoint presentations to these deep schools of fish."

This hybrid Carolina rigging/cranking tactic has proved especially productive for bass suspended off bluffs, dams and bridge pilings. But it will also work in situations where there is cover like brushpiles and stumps (using a depthfinder to present the bait above or adjacent to the cover).

"As the bait seems to just sit in one place, the current will make it kind of shimmy back and forth like suspended baitfish do," Potts says. "Most of the strikes come when the bait is stationary.

"You hardly ever feel the fish strike the bait. They just seem to swim off with it. It's almost the same feeling you get when a bass hits a Fluke or Slug-Go-type bait. It just gets heavy, or you see your line moving one way or the other."

Despite dealing with suspended bass situations, this technique has produced as many as 30 bass a day, as well as 20-pound stringers in Texas tournaments for Potts and David.

"The frustrating thing about suspended bass is that you might see a big school sitting off a bluff or point, but you normally have to wait until they come all the way up before you can catch them," Chad Potts says. "But you might have to wait from 8 in the morning until 3 in the afternoon before they come up.

"With this technique, you don't have to wait."

MAKING THE BAIT strike the bottom is a must when fishing with big crankbaits in shallow water.

OVERGUNNING WITH CRANKBAITS

A big crankbait makes for a full meal for big, hungry bass

W HEN IT COMES to bass fishing, a little "old school" thinking is not a bad idea. Faced with an ever widening array of lures and tactics, sometimes just getting back to the basics can help sort through the haze. Then again, there are times when "old school" is just plain "old."

For instance, the traditional logic in crankbait fishing has always been to select a lure that will dive just deep enough to tick the top of the cover or structure being fished. However, this cornerstone of cranking was developed back when lure depth ranges were fairly limited, and crankbait strategies filled a thin volume of bass fishing knowledge.

As fishermen began to experiment and the lures they used improved, the strict guidelines of crankbait warfare expanded. For professionals like Skeet Reese, Todd Faircloth and Mark Menendez, mismatching crankbaits to water depth — especially in the shallows — has become less an exception and more the rule.

(Opposite page) BE ON GUARD in the seconds after a crankbait has deflected off an object. The strike will happen at any moment.

EFFICIENCY

"As a general rule of thumb, you want a bait that will be in contact with the bottom at all times. If you want to slow the retrieve and let the bait float up a bit, you want that option," notes Reese, a Californian who has proved his fishing skills nationwide on the BASS tour.

"Even with a deep diving crankbait, often the problem is that it typically reaches its maximum depth halfway back to the boat. So, you have a lot of wasted ground where the bait isn't hitting the stumps or brushpiles or gravel; places where you want it to be."

While anglers have recognized this inherent inefficiency of crankbaits, the common response was simply

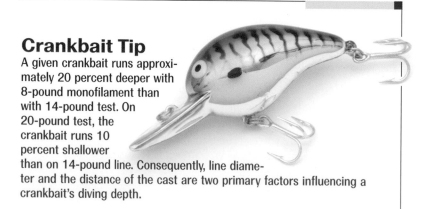

Crankbait Tip

A given crankbait runs approximately 20 percent deeper with 8-pound monofilament than with 14-pound test. On 20-pound test, the crankbait runs 10 percent shallower than on 14-pound line. Consequently, line diameter and the distance of the cast are two primary factors influencing a crankbait's diving depth.

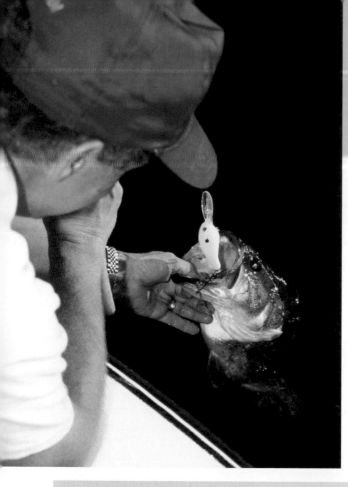

CHOOSE A CRANKBAIT designed to run roughly 2 feet deeper than the existing depth to keep the bait in the strike zone.

to make long casts to expand coverage or reduce line size to dive deeper. Even so, the gains generated were minimal, at best. Moreover, the lure was operating at its maximum depth range, which didn't allow for much creative lure control in prime target areas.

In facing up to this dilemma, professionals like Reese have increasingly relied on crankbaits that dive demonstrably deeper than their intended targets. As Reese puts it, "Why throw a shallow diver that may only hit three stumps, when I can use a deeper diver, adjust my retrieve and hit 10 of them?"

GETTING A GRIP

For Todd Faircloth, a Texas pro who cut his angling teeth on the likes of Sam Rayburn and Toledo Bend, a prime objective of overgunning with crankbaits comes by way of lure control.

Instead of matching a crankbait to the water depth and working the

Brushing Crankbaits

For most bass fishermen, brush and treble hooks just don't mix. For Kentucky pro Mark Menendez, though, it's simply a matter of having the right recipe.

"The problem with crankbaits in brush is twofold: One is presentation, which means actually putting the lure in there and fighting through the brush. Two is being scared of throwing a $5 lure and perhaps never seeing it again," observes Menendez.

"These are the things that prevent us from using crankbaits in shallow cover."

The answer to both parts of the riddle comes in solving the presentation issue, he says, which means limiting one's casting distance and targeting rather small and very specific areas.

Traditionally, long casts coupled with a steady or stop-and-go retrieve is what produces crankbait success. In shallow, cover-oriented situations, however, depth is not an issue. In general, Menendez focuses on water less than 5 feet deep and frequently only 2 or 3 feet in depth.

Instead of a straight, consistent retrieve, he opts for lure movement that more closely resembles a jerkbait twitch-

and-jerk presentation. By jerking the lure down with short, rapid twitches, Menendez not only avoids plowing his crankbait into brushy tangles, but he also keeps it in the strike zone longer.

"This retrieve keeps the bait in a very active state and a short distance from the boat. Most of my casts are less than 50 feet. They're very short presentations because I'm only fishing specific sections of that shallow cover.

"Many times, you're making presentations in areas that are the size of garbage

can lids. Basically, you're putting a crankbait in the same places as a spinnerbait, buzzbait or jig. When you find the key zone, you have to keep it there as long as possible."

In this technique, every cast produces a different presentation. By adjusting his speed of retrieve and rod angle, Menendez can feel and finesse his way under, over and through the cover. In some cases, it may require lifting the bait to avoid a nasty tangle or simply letting the lure float up and over a snag.

lure briefly through a small window of opportunity, Faircloth often relies on a high rod position to keep a deeper diving plug at the optimum depth. Held at the 10 or 12 o'clock position, he uses his rod to keep a 6-foot crankbait running along at 4 feet and still have some options regarding retrieve speed. To better understand what is going on down there, Faircloth generally chooses a crankbait that will run 2 feet deeper than the water he is fishing.

But far from relying solely on this mechanical means of controlling depth, the young Texan also experiments with line diameter, using heavier sizes to limit depth, and smaller tests to increase it. Although he does admit that fluorocarbon line will get deeper than monofilament, he prefers mono because it offers better depth control.

Of special significance to Faircloth is the ability of these deeper diving crankbaits to trigger strikes from isolated brushpiles and stumps. Rather than bump along at a steady depth until he runs his bait into the target, he brings the lure down from above.

"The fish are watching the bait approach them, then all of a sudden it's banging around in their home. It's an aggressive, power fishing technique," offers Faircloth.

"But with a crankbait, it's not actually when you hit the cover, but when the bait comes out of the cover. That's when about 75 percent of your bites come on a crankbait."

RAISING A RUCKUS

In addition to the increased time spent in the strike zone, a deeper diving crankbait also creates a commotion on the bottom that is often the difference in

1 — Path of a crankbait matched to water depth. 2 — Path of a crankbait "overgunned" to water depth. 3 — Distance lure is in effective strike zone when matched to water depth. 4 — Expanded distance lure is in strike zone when "overgunned" to depth.

With a high rod position from 10 to 12 o'clock, the maximum depth of the crankbait can be controlled. Upgrading in-line diameter can enhance this.

In targeting isolated cover, Todd Faircloth will crank the lure at a shallower depth, then dive the bait down to and through the cover.

One of the overlooked advantages to "overgunning" crankbaits is in their ability to locate isolated structure and key structure areas.

The Hooking Connection

With two sets of trebles and constant pressure down the line, it seems inconceivable that a bass could actually dislodge itself from a crankbait. Yet, according to Texas pro Clark Wendlandt, it is probably the worst lure in terms of losing fish.

"A lot of it has to do with how fish strike the bait. On some days, the bass may be inhaling it — with the lure actually inside their mouth. But, those days are a rarity."

Although a fisherman can't do much about how a bass strikes the lure, he can do something when it comes to hook sets. In fact, Wendlandt believes that improper hook setting is probably the most common problem affecting crankbait anglers.

"You need to let the fish load up on the bait and basically let the fish set the hook on himself. It's not like a worm or spinnerbait, where you're jerking hard.

"At the same time, I'm going to try to keep the fish from jumping. The only way to do that is to keep your rod down and, if necessary, lower it into the water."

Determining the amount of pressure to use during the fight is somewhat of a balancing act between being forceful and being deliberate, admits Wendlandt. Around heavy cover, the primary objective is to get them away from the tangle, delivering enough pressure to turn the fish, even at the expense of losing it. Allowing a crankbait fish to get amongst the cover where the exposed hooks can snag easily is a battle where the bass nearly always come out on top.

In open water situations, it's a much harder call. While the goal is to be deliberate and not force the issue, there may be unseen objects that will end the fight prematurely. Obviously, the more an angler knows about what lies underneath the surface, the better judgments can be made in how delicately or forcefully to fight a fish.

triggering strikes. This can be particularly effective when fishing pressure has turned bass off to standard presentations.

"A bass is naturally curious and, after seeing 50 crankbaits go through an area just ticking the cover, a lure that churns up the bottom will pick off one or two of the most aggressive fish," counsels Menendez.

"We are creatures of habit. What was successful a day, a week or a year ago makes us relish what we once had. We sometimes get locked into things that once were successful. By being radically different, a deeper diving crankbait in shallow water will get their attention."

By choosing a deeper diving crankbait, an angler can also increase the size of the lure and, in doing so, upgrade the size of the fish being caught. A larger profile crankbait will also attract the attention of larger fish in an area by magnifying the effect of an unusual presentation, says Menendez.

DIGGING DEEPER

While overgunning your crankbaits can pay dividends throughout the year, perhaps the most obvious application is during the prespawn, when big fish are up and moving through the shallows.

"In the prespawn, daddy is moving up to the bushes looking for a place to make a bed, and momma is still hanging out at the women's club waiting for conditions to get right. This is when you will have those bigger fish in that shallower zone," notes Menendez.

"A creek channel or grassline leading into a spawning area would be the perfect scenario."

For Reese, a key reason for this prespawn response is the focus on crawfish as a primary forage for bass.

"By tearing up the bottom, stirring up mud and turning over rocks, you're producing the effect of crawfish coming out of hibernation. In the prespawn — especially with bigger females — that's the key forage. A deeper diving crankbait gives the same effect as a jig or Carolina rig, plus you can cover water faster and really pinpoint the fish."

In warmer water situations, such as postspawn and summer, the bottom-churning action of a crankbait can produce even better results, observes Faircloth, particularly when fished quickly around brushpiles and stumps.

"In the summer, bass have to feed to survive. The fish are a lot more aggressive, and there is more baitfish activity. Everything is more active. In most situations where I've found that

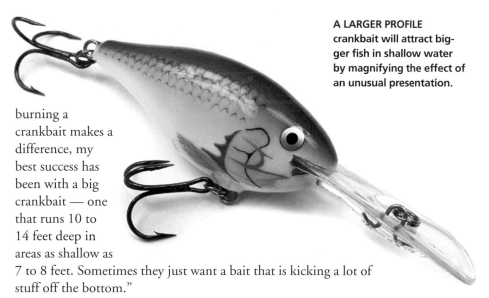

A LARGER PROFILE crankbait will attract bigger fish in shallow water by magnifying the effect of an unusual presentation.

What's The Hang-up?

Perhaps the greatest source of resistance in overgunning with crankbaits comes from anglers who either fear losing baits or don't want to waste time having to constantly unfoul bottom glop from their lures.

On the first point, Todd Faircloth responds that crankbaits with larger bills actually can negotiate cover better than shallow runners. Since he prefers using Stanford cedar crankbaits, he hedges his bets with lures that can float away from tangles much easier. While Skeet Reese opts for the plastic-molded Lucky Craft CB Series, he shrugs off these concerns because the presence of most obstructions is telegraphed up through the line. "Anyway," he laughs, "that's what they make lure retrievers for."

On the subject of fouling baits, there is no getting around the fact that a firm bottom is a prerequisite in making overgunning work. However, the flip side of the coin is that by using deeper diving crankbaits to first locate hard bottom areas, the technique provides two important services — first in locating key areas, and then catching the fish that live there.

"This method allows me to fish a flat or hump and find what is down there. I can fish a lot more water to find the right type of cover," notes Reese.

burning a crankbait makes a difference, my best success has been with a big crankbait — one that runs 10 to 14 feet deep in areas as shallow as 7 to 8 feet. Sometimes they just want a bait that is kicking a lot of stuff off the bottom."

As he does in the spring, Menendez also looks for this aggressive presentation to produce bigger bass in the postspawn and summer periods. While practicing for a Lake Eufaula tournament, Menendez once played his big fish card to perfection after locating fish on the corners of main lake points.

"Anywhere I could find a corner out in front of a bay — whether it was the corner of a main lake point with a piece of wood on it, some standing timber, or it was a corner of a creek channel — it didn't matter. Anywhere I could find a corner, I found bass. It got so easy," recalls Menendez.

"Most of this was in 7 to 8 feet of water, and I could just hit the top of it with a Fat Free Jr. But I picked up the wrong rod and made about three casts with a Fat Free Sr., whacked a piece of wood, and a 4-pounder ate it. I started throwing that Fat Free Sr. at every 7- to 8-foot corner I could find. In about an hour and a half, I had about 30 pounds."

Later in the year, overgunning with crankbaits can yield similar results, especially when high pressure or weather fronts make the fish less active and a fisherman needs something extra to stimulate reaction strikes. Even in prime fall conditions, when bass are actively pursuing baitfish, the sheer audacity of this power presentation separates a crankbait from the clouds of baitfish.

"At times, you'll get so many shad confined to a small area, why would a bass ever bite something that wasn't real? This approach is so radically different, it gets their attention," counsels Menendez.

TUNING BASICS FOR CRANKBAITS

Fishing without tuning your lures is like deer hunting without sighting in your rifle

I F YOU COULD somehow observe each bass fisherman who uses crankbaits, you would probably see that most simply tie on a lure and begin "chucking and winding."

And most will catch a few fish that way. But if your idea of crankbait fishing is to take a lure out of the package, tie it on and cast it out, you may be settling for less than the best performance from these time-proven lures.

To get the most out of crankbait fishing, you have to do your homework — that is, even before heading for the lake, you need to make sure

the lures you intend to use are performing the way they were intended.

An expert on the subject is Tom Seward, a veteran lure designer for Worden's Lures/ Yakima Bait Co. in Granger, Wash. Seward's useful insight is an asset for making crankbaits run true to fully exploit their potential.

"The simple step of tuning a crankbait is so important and so basic that I have a hard time understanding how a professional fisherman or a serious weekend angler can make a trip without knowing the exact status and condition of each crankbait in his or her tacklebox," he says.

Adds Seward, "Even after 20 years of designing and working with these lures, I make sure I am never on the water with an unchecked, untuned lure."

A competitive fisherman knows that losing a single fish because his hooks aren't sharp can be extremely detrimental to tournament standings. But did you ever consider the costs of fishing a poorly tuned bait?

Regardless of claims that a bait is "tank tested" or "runs straight right out of the package," if you typically fish your crankbaits without checking them, you are settling for less than the best performance from your lures.

WHAT TO LOOK FOR

What are you missing by fishing an untried lure? Here are a few possibilities, according to Tom Seward:

■ *Maximum vibration* — "I rate vibration (action) as the most important design factor.

A crankbait running on its side at speed will never produce its intended action. I have never had a fish take a free-running crankbait that was badly out of tune — no exceptions."

According to Seward, in companies that tank-test lures, a good tank-tester can actually feel the change in an out-of-tune lure without looking in the test tank. "This ability is a reason I often have these people test new designs for vibration," Seward points out.

Fish perceive crankbaits visually and through their built-in vibration as potential prey in distress or flight, he says. When perfectly tuned, the best crankbaits simulate fear, distress and flight to a predatory fish. This is a very powerful stimulus, and tuned, well-designed lures produce this without ever hitting the bottom or deflecting off cover.

■ *Speed control* — "On a very slow retrieve, your out-of-tune lure might track OK. But speed it up, and it will swim to one side and lean over at the back, presenting an unnatural appearance to fish. After a certain degree of departure from a straight line, it simply will not get a strike. This is especially critical in clear water, where speed is essential in making fish take a hard bait. Speed is what crankbaits are all about, and you do not want to ignore this major design function."

■ *Maximum diving depth* — "This is especially critical in deep diving lures. A deep running

Crankbait Tip

As a general rule, wide wobbling lures are better in warm or stained water conditions, while tight wobbling crankbaits are more suited to cold or clear water. By changing to a different crankbait action, an angler can often improve the quality of the strike.

Assessing Crankbait Bites

OK, so you've got the bait tuned and ready to send on the hunt. And if you are like many crankbait users, there has always been — and always will be — a desire to know precisely how bass are responding to the lure.

The accuracy of those guesses is determined by the amount of information a fisherman can glean from each strike. With crankbaits in particular, the way a bass strikes the lure is often an open book to how the lure should be retrieved, if changes to color or action are required, and the aggression level of the bass themselves.

However, before an angler starts evaluating strikes, he must first be consistent in his hook setting efforts. With a more parabolic rod that doesn't telegraph a strike too rapidly, a fisherman does not respond too quickly, thereby allowing the fish to fully engulf the lure.

Unfortunately, this describes the best-case scenario. More commonly, bass are hooked in any number of ways — around the mouth, side of the head or by a single hook.

To accurately assess a bite, BASS touring pro Ray Sedgwick first tries to determine the aggressiveness of the strike.

"If they push the bait toward you, hitting it extremely hard, you're giving them pretty much what they want in terms of lure action, color and size.

"When they slap at it, you might hook them in the side of the head. If you have sensitive line, you can actually feel fish turn at a bait and miss it. Most of the time, these fish are just butting and slapping at the lure and not really trying to eat it. They're not necessarily feeding, but they're in a mood to kill."

In stained water, one way to correct the slapping and butting of the bait is by switching to a rattling crankbait. With the added noise, a bass is alerted much sooner to the crankbait's presence, and the fish can get a much more accurate fix on the lure's position as it moves through the strike zone.

In clear water, the strike response is largely a visual one, so an overly loud rattle might stimulate exactly the opposite reaction desired: Instead of being attracted to the lure, the fish may be repelled.

crankbait that is slightly out of tune might appear to run straight, but it actually travels in a wide arc beneath the surface, keeping it above the intended strike zone."

■ *Trolling performance* — "Although trolling is not permissible in tournament situations, the practice is very useful for locating fish and for determining their positions on large structures. And if you troll for other species, an out-of-tune lure will barrel-roll after contacting the bottom and will often broach the surface — wasting your time as it tries to track back to depth. In addition, you will face a loss of speed control, and 'power trolling' will be out of the question."

All of the above factors should convince you of the importance of checking and tuning every crankbait you intend to fish, according to Seward. What's more, tuning is so simple that it can give an edge to any Bassmaster who wants to develop and improve the skills that will take him to the next level.

WHERE TO TUNE

If you have access to a swimming pool — either yours or a neighbor's — you have it made. If not, there may be other options, advises Seward.

Almost equal to a swimming pool is a dock extending over clear water, especially water deep enough to let you check your deep divers. A spot out of strong winds is best, and it must be away from any current.

Bring as many lures as you think you can stand to tune, and be prepared to spend the time to do the job right.

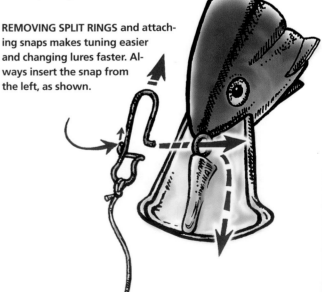

REMOVING SPLIT RINGS and attaching snaps makes tuning easier and changing lures faster. Always insert the snap from the left, as shown.

Learning The Simple Basics Of Crankbaiting

WHAT YOU WILL SEE

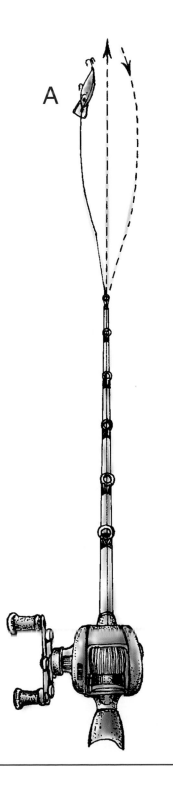

A

WHAT YOU CAN DO

FRONT VIEW
SHALLOW RUNNER

B

DEEP DIVER

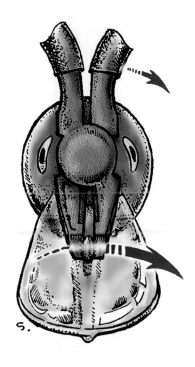

S.

AVOID TWISTING THE STAINLESS LINE TIE IN LURE'S NOSE OR LIP!

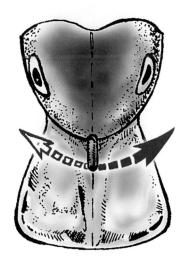

CAUTIOUSLY BEND EYE AS IF ON A HINGE! AVOID ANY TWIST IF POSSIBLE.

DEEP DIVER FRONT VIEW

BEND THE LINE TIE IN THE DIRECTION YOU WANT THE LURE TO GO. ALWAYS THINK ABOUT A HINGE AND MAKE MICRO-MOVEMENTS WITH THE PLIERS.

BE SURE TO TEST your lures at or above the retrieve speeds you intend to use them. Doing so beforehand will free up more time for fishing.

"I suggest testing most lures on a rod and reel spooled with 14- to 17-pound-test mono," he says. "Heavier line restricts diving depth and saves valuable time. Bring along a cardboard box with the top cut off, so you can hang tuned lures along the edge."

To adjust the lures' line ties, you'll also need a set of pliers, including long-nosed pliers, small pliers and square-jawed pliers. A permanent marker is helpful for marking the lips of special lures to help you identify them later.

TUNING BASICS

With a little practice, tuning is fairly easy.

Simply cast the lure out and wind it back with smooth, steady pressure. Be sure to test your lures at or above the retrieve speeds you intend to crank them. You can't tune your lures correctly at a low, casual cranking speed — learn how they perform at higher rates of retrieve.

As the lure swims back to you, sight down your rod as though it were a rifle, noting whether the bait swims to the right or left.

To tune the lure, hold it in your hand with its nose pointing toward you. Using the type of pliers that best fits your lure, very carefully bend — never twist — the line tie in the direction you want the lure to go. For example, if the lure is running off to the left of your rod tip, bend the line tie slightly to the right.

The Art Of Covering Water

Understanding a concept and being able to act on it are sometimes two very different things. This is particularly true when bass fishermen are forced to "cover water" or shift into that fast-forward search mode of finding and eliminating water.

However, covering water cannot be a random exercise, "a blind chunk-and-wind deal," according to BASS touring pro Kenyon Hill.

"Covering water is the search mode," he explains. "The biggest mistake made by fishermen is how they decide where to go and where to start. For me, it's no different than fishing a tournament — I make a game plan when I'm trying to cover water."

To avoid a long day of casting practice, lure selection needs to be simpli-

fied. First and foremost, choose a confidence crankbait, one that has been proved over time. Second, based on the seasonal pattern and prevailing conditions, select a lure that can effectively work the depth range you expect to be most productive. Since the diving capabilities of many crankbaits are overstated on the package, Hill chooses a bait that can easily make contact with the bottom or with objects at a certain depth.

Third, stay with traditional colors such as firetiger (which resembles sunfish and other natural forage) and Tennessee shad. Being overly cover conscious early in the game can only hamper your efficiency in covering water. A proven lure pattern fished in the right water color will generate enough strikes to let you know where fish are located. While it may not be the absolutely perfect choice, the search process is not the time to make those subtle adjustments.

Hold the lure with your hands close to your body for firm, tight, minute motions with the pliers. Practice will give you the right touch.

"Always bend the stainless steel line ties as if they were on a hinge, and avoid twisting them," recommends Seward. "Screw eyes can be twisted to tune a lure, but I do this as a last resort, and I like to epoxy them in place before fishing them."

IT'S A SNAP

If you want your lure to run properly, use a snap. Some anglers with a lot of time on the water still do not use snaps, preferring split rings on their crankbaits. Others are just not aware of the advantages of snaps, or they think that because a split ring was installed at the factory, that's the way things are supposed to be.

The top reason for using a snap is speed. Speed is what makes you an efficient angler in wind, current and other fishing situations. Quick lure changes dominate other considerations on the water. To change lure color or size when using a split ring, you must retie each time and cut the line twice. A snap allows changes in seconds, or by the time you finish this sentence.

Snaps are far superior to split rings when it comes to tuning a lure. The thick, double-wire loop of the split ring is a tuning nightmare, and it forces the pliers away from the line tie, often causing distorted, bent or twisted line ties. A snap lies flat in most cases and lets you get the pliers right down to the base of the line tie — a major advantage.

Snaps do not have a groove or split area to catch on the line tie like split rings. The notch, or break, in the split ring can catch, giving you a false impression of an erratic or out-of-tune lure.

Never use a swivel with a snap. This is unnecessary and represents the use of extra terminal tackle. It gives lures a heavy "hardware" look.

"Some fishermen worry about the snap opening up and costing them a fish," notes Seward. "In fact, this is the No. 1 question I hear regarding snaps. I can remember just about every fish I lost in the last 20 years because of snaps: a total of three."

You do have to retie occasionally, because the line will become abraded, especially when fighting fish. It's a good idea to retie every one-half to two hours. Always, always use a knot with a double loop around the snap. A Palomar knot is unbeatable.

CHECK YOUR BAITS

While you're tuning your lures, be sure to check each one for loose components, leaks and dull hooks. Repair or discard any bait that doesn't measure up.

The tuning/checking process might take a few hours, depending on how many lures you're testing, but it will be time well spent.

Do your homework, and you'll never again have to wonder, "Is it in tune or isn't it?" After all, you have more valuable things to do when you're fishing — such as locating fish and figuring out the best lures and retrieves — than worry about whether your lure is performing correctly under the water.

KEEP CRANKBAITS in tune so they will appear more natural in the water.

SWEEP THE ROD tip slowly upward or to the side to achieve the action required to worm a crankbait.

WORMING WITH A CRANKBAIT

Add this unusual tactic to your repertoire of crankbait retrieves

FROM A DISTANCE, Ohioan Gary Dees appears to be fishing a plastic worm. He holds his rod tip high and works the bait through the edge of a logjam with alternating pulls and pauses. As he reels in and makes another cast, the lure flashes in the sun. Was that a crankbait?

A closer look confirms this to be true. If Dees were not one of the Buckeye State's most accomplished tournament anglers, you wouldn't give it a second thought. But now you just have to know why he fishes a crankbait in such an unusual manner.

(Opposite page) WORM A suspending crankbait during the extremes of hot and cold weather. This is the time when bass become lethargic, and they need cajoling.

Dees maintains a conventional low rod position when he wants a crankbait to reach its maximum depth. When cranking cover, however, he can present the lure more efficiently and endure fewer snags by sweeping the rod tip slowly upward or to the side. The motion is similar to that used when retrieving a plastic worm along the bottom.

The high rod helps Dees feel the cover and also stop, pause and give slack line as the lure bumps over and around various objects. It's also an effective method for coaxing temperamental bass into action.

"I've been doing that since I started fishing crankbaits with a 7-foot rod," says Dees. "The long rod lets me control the bait better, and I can even use it to pitch into places that would be hard to hit with regular casting gear. A lot of guys like fiberglass rods for crankbaits, but I get better control with a medium action Berkley graphite rod."

WORMING WITH LIPPED LURES

After casting and cranking the lure into the cover, Dees raises his rod tip, which pulls the crankbait down and ahead. When the lure bumps a limb, the bottom or some other object, Dees stops, drops the rod tip and takes up slack. Then he gently sweeps the rod up and repeats the process until the lure clears the cover or dupes a bass.

"When you move a crankbait with a high rod tip," says Dees, "you can feel what's happening a lot better than when your rod is pointing right at

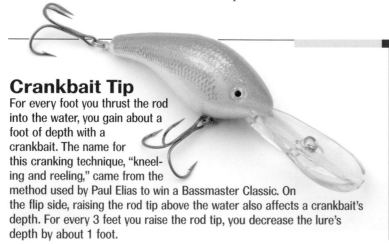

Crankbait Tip

For every foot you thrust the rod into the water, you gain about a foot of depth with a crankbait. The name for this cranking technique, "kneeling and reeling," came from the method used by Paul Elias to win a Bassmaster Classic. On the flip side, raising the rod tip above the water also affects a crankbait's depth. For every 3 feet you raise the rod tip, you decrease the lure's depth by about 1 foot.

Bill Dance's Worming Tackle (For Crankbaits)

The debate over using fiberglass and graphite rods for crankbaiting goes on. But for Bill Dance, the choice is graphite, especially when he worms a crankbait.

"I go with a long, medium action graphite Quantum rod because the sensitivity of graphite is especially beneficial with the horizontal jigging method — it makes strike detection easier."

Dance matches the rod with a 4.4:1 gear ratio Quantum baitcasting reel. The slow gear ratio provides more power for retrieving big crankbaits and makes it easier to impart the slow to moderate speeds that allow these lures to dig as deep as possible.

"This reel also gives you the advantage of leveraging a big bass with its slower gear ratio," he adds. "And the chances are that you'll need it, considering the size of some of the bass that suspend and can be caught on this technique.

"I don't get them every time," says Dance, "but horizontal jigging with a Suspending Fat Free Shad works better on suspended bass than any other technique I've ever used."

the lure. And you can move the bait to one side or the other. That helps you finagle it through cover. A change of direction also triggers bites."

A neutral buoyancy crankbait matches well with this "worming" technique because it hangs in place or rises slowly during pauses. You have more control and can let the lure linger in the strike zone longer than with a highly buoyant crankbait that quickly floats up.

MARK DAVIS DOES IT

Lest you think worming a crankbait is too far afield to be worthy of consideration, take note that Mark Davis employed this method when he won the 1995 Bassmaster Classic at North Carolina's High Rock Lake. Davis' primary targets were tall, dense brushpiles 8 to 10 feet deep, adorned with old fishing line.

The large crankbait Davis relied on, the Excalibur Series Fat Free Shad, digs as deep as 18 feet. To reduce the lure's depth, and to prevent breaking off, Davis opted for 20-pound monofilament. Because the crankbait is a floater-diver, Davis worked it with sideways sweeps of his rod to keep the lure down in the cover.

"When Excalibur introduced the Suspending Fat Free Shad," says Davis, "worming a crankbait got a whole lot easier. With a suspending bait, you can hold your rod tip high. There's a lot to be said for that. First, you gain a lot of feel. And when you pull a bait instead of reel it, you know exactly how far and fast it's moving. It gives you more control and lets you put a lot of erratic action on the bait. You can slow it down, stop it; show the fish something they haven't seen."

Davis worms a suspending crankbait most often during the extremes of hot and cold weather, because this is when bass grow lethargic and need a little extra cajoling. Once he gets the lure down in what he feels is the strike zone, he may let it hover in place for several seconds and give it short twitches. He thinks of this ploy as finesse crankbait fishing. You must be alert, just as with worm fishing, to detect strikes.

"A lot of strikes feel much the same as when you're reeling a crankbait," he says. "But sometimes, when the lure is hanging in place, you feel only a little tick or peck. You may have to drop the rod tip and take up slack before setting the hook. But don't slam the hooks home like you do with a jig or worm. Just pull back firmly and maintain steady pressure."

BILL DANCE DOES IT, TOO

Television personality Bill Dance, another advocate of worming a crankbait, also prefers no-nonsense bottom contact. In water 12 feet or deeper, he opts for the BD7 Fat Free Shad, which runs 14 to 18 feet deep. He drops down to the BD6, which runs 10 to 14 feet, when fishing water 6 to 11 feet deep. In water less than 6 feet deep, he goes with a BD5 that runs 8 to 10 feet.

"I make four or five fast turns to get the bait started," says Dance, "then continue

GARY DEES uses a D Bait because of the flat-sided balsa lure's high buoyancy properties.

cranking with a slow-to-moderate retrieve until it hits the bottom. At that point, I stop and work the crankbait about like I would a worm or a jig-and-pork. I'll twitch the rod tip from about 10 o'clock to 11 o'-clock, take up slack line real quick and let the bait sit right on the bottom. It looks just like an injured baitfish struggling along. I cannot tell you how effective that is. At times, bass knock the fire out of it when it is just sitting still."

In most instances, believes Dance, bass that suspend above bottom and away from structure or cover are just hanging out between meals. They're in a neutral mood and won't move far or fast to take a bait. To catch them, you must dangle a lure right in their faces and needle them into striking.

This is when Dance ties on a shad pattern Suspending Fat Free Shad that runs at the same depth as, or a little above, a school of bass he has located with his depthfinder. He makes a long cast over the school and cranks the lure down just as when fishing a bottom structure. When he figures the lure has attained its maximum depth, he stops reeling and lets the bait hover in place.

"I may let it remain in a suspended state 5 to 10 seconds," says Dance, "then I'll 'horizontal jig' it with my rod in about the 10 o'clock position. Then I'll wait and twitch it again. If they don't like that, I'll make three quick cranks on the reel and stop it again. I keep the bait right in amongst them and try different actions until I make one bust it. Sometimes they hit it when it's dead-still."

When he does catch a bass, Dance remembers the nuances of the retrieve that triggered the strike, something at which he excels. He then repeats the same presentation. Strikes are often slow in coming, but Dance knows that with persistence he can catch bass that would otherwise elude him.

To find suspended bass, Dance starts searching near a ledge or some other structure that attracts the bass when they're in a feeding mode. If the edge of the drop breaks from, say, 15 to 30 feet of water, Dance knows the bass are likely to suspend about 15 feet deep so they can move straight to the break when the dinner bell rings.

"If I can't find bass on the ledge," says Dance, "I start idling slowly in a tight circle and look for them with my depthfinder. They might be only 10 feet away, or they could be more than 30 yards from that key bottom feature. I'll gradually widen my circles until I spot them. When I do, I quickly take landmarks and get to work with a Suspending Fat Free Shad."

BILL DANCE tries various retrieves and rod sweeps until he finds the method preferred by the bass. Then, he applies the nuances of the retrieve to other areas for catching deep bass.

LIPLESS CRANKS

Lipless Lures Are Good
For More Than Chunking
And Winding …

BECAUSE IT resembles a shad, the lipless crankbait is a deadly weapon for trolling.

TROLLING LIPLESS CRANKBAITS

Try this unconventional approach to trophy hunting with lipless crankbaits

WHAT STARTED AS A frivolous Florida fishing fling for a paltry few anglers turned into a deadly fishing technique with a fanatical following. The technique is a ridiculously simple one . . . so simple, in fact, that many sophisticated Bassmasters refused to try it — until they saw bass catches being made with it.

"Basically, all the fishermen do is troll along the edges of weeds and flooded cypress knees with lipless crankbaits, and they catch bass. Lots of 'em. And they're big!" says Ernest Wigglesworth, owner of McGilvray's Fish Camp on 4,000-acre Newnans Lake in north-central Florida near Gainesville. "For years, a lot of our best fishermen have been catching big bass with small, lipless crankbaits, like Rat-L-Traps, that imitate shad. But often they'd cast all day and boat just three or four fish. That got some of our regular anglers thinking about a better way of fishing the same lures in the same places where they caught bigmouth."

What a handful of Newnans Lake fishermen determined to do was troll the lipless lures along the lake's shoreline edges. And what they discovered was one of the most deadly fish-catching methods to come along in years.

While many of these anglers tried to keep the technique quiet, big catches of big bass eventually got plenty of attention. Heavyweight catches became so commonplace on Newnans during the hot, broiling days of late spring and summer — a time when many Florida anglers have trouble catching any decent fish — that newspaper reports of such catches ran almost constantly.

(Opposite page) BEFORE THEY'VE had the chance to be selective, big bass will nail a lipless crankbait as it speeds by their lair.

Crankbait Tip

Lipless crankbaits are perfect for targeting schooling bass. They can be cast far and make a lot of noise — two qualities that are beneficial when chasing schoolies. To improve the odds of landing these unpredictable fish, make long casts and "burn" the lure so it runs just under the surface.

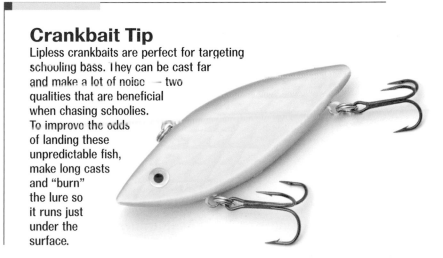

Naturally, as the technique caught on with anglers, it spread to other Florida waters. Soon, big catches of heavyweight largemouth were being made by anglers trolling lipless crankbaits on Rodman Reservoir, Lake George, the St. Johns River, the Harris and Tsala-Apopka chains of lakes, many small lakes in the Ocala National Forest, on famed Lake Kissimmee, and West Lake Tohopekaliga.

Within months, trollers working lipless lures were scoring well on largemouth as far south as Lake Okeechobee and as far west as Lake Talquin. Some anglers also began employing the technique successfully in the bass rich rivers of Georgia and on some of that state's impoundments, such as Clarks Hill Reservoir, Lake Lanier and Lake Blackshear.

Like most effective fishing techniques, this one can be simple or complicated, depending on how much an angler intends to work at the method.

To the occasional fisherman, it's a godsend, since it is a no-brainer method of catching plenty of good-size fish. They simply tie on the lures, flip them behind the boat, and roar off down the lake — catching bass and most anything else that swims in their wakes.

For the sophisticated angler, trolling the little lipless lures takes consummate skill and great attention to detail. It requires manipulating many trolling nuances, any of which can bring additional bassin' success to any day on the water.

Seasoned bass anglers quickly recognized that trolling lipless lures along shoreline cover and over submerged weedbeds, like hydrilla and coontail moss, was the fastest means of checking such waters for largemouth.

It is deadly around other shallow structure, too, such as riprap, bulkheads, pier pilings and bridge abutments. What is more, it's a fast method of fishing. Speed in working such areas is especially important during hot or bright weather, since under those conditions the bulk of the best fishing is had at daybreak and dusk. So the quicker an angler can cover a lily pad-lined or cypress-studded shoreline, the sooner he finds feeding fish during the optimum hours of the day. Too, on days when bass are finicky and scattered, trolling crankbaits results in more fish per hour spent on the water.

Lipless crankbaits are ideal for shallow water bass fishing for several reasons. The baits are shaped like favorite forage of largemouth bass — shad and shiners. Too, slow sinking lipless lures tend to "plane" during trolling, rather than dive deep like crankbaits sporting diving bills or "lips." So, with lipless lures, Florida fishermen are able to quickly check very shallow, weedy, cover-filled shallows where diving crankbaits with lips would hang up.

For example, during a typical trolling pass with a lipless lure, an angler would speed up to get his plug over a high spot in hydrilla, but would slow down to allow his lure to fall a bit when he checked deeper water or the dropoff of a weedbed.

Some anglers modify their lures, adding slip sinker weights ahead of the lures for deeper trolling. They use bullet weights up to 1 ounce, which they slip onto the fishing line, then tie on a barrel swivel, a 2- to 3-foot leader and the lure. Others drill holes in the baits and fill them with weights, or merely allow them to fill with water during fishing.

THE LONG HANDLES of flipping rods make trolling and landing big fish easier on lipless crankbaits.

For very shallow trolling, some fishermen use streamlined, cigar-shaped cork floats ahead of lipless crankbaits to make them run just inches under the surface. This proves deadly when fishing slightly submerged hydrilla weeds, which are prime forage areas for giant largemouth. Many anglers working dense weedbeds also remove the forward treble hook of a lipless crankbait and replace the rear treble with a single, short-shank hook or a wire weedguard hook. This greatly reduces lure-fouling in cover and often results in boating more bass, because the fish are less likely to tangle exposed hooks in grass, logs or brush.

Trolling lipless crankbaits is basically a shallow water technique, since the lures do not dive down at higher speeds like other crankbaits. Bottom-bumping crankbaits have been the mainstay of many trollers for decades, so the use of free-swimming plugs for trolling is dubiously looked at by some veteran fishermen.

Some very successful anglers pump their rods when trolling lipless lures. By pulling, yanking or pumping the rod irregularly during trolling, the angler is imparting an extra bit of darting-and-falling action to the trolled plug. Pulling on the rod gives the lure a spurt of speed and causes it to move up and forward. By dropping the rod tip back down, the lure's forward progress slows, so it falls. When the line comes tight again due to the forward speed of trolling, the lure zips back up. This zigzag, sawtoothed lure pattern triggers bass into striking out of instinct.

A quick change in rod angle or boat path also can incite bass to hit, especially during the dog days of summer. The theory behind this trolling tactic is that bass frequently will follow the lure, apparently undecided about whether to strike. But a sudden dart in a different direction elicits an immediate strike response from the bass.

The same explanation applies when anglers "speed-troll" lipless lures. A crankbait ripping along at break-neck speed causes bass — particularly bass lying in the edge of heavy cover such as weedbeds, stumpflats, submerged brush and undercut river banks — to hit the lure instantly, without allowing it time to look over the lure like it could a slow moving plastic worm or topwater plug. The fish doesn't have time to be selective. It simply reacts.

While many trollers prefer using standard, short, stiff-action "worm rods," some have learned that long popping rods or flipping sticks are better. The greater length of such rods lets anglers work trolled plugs better around cover edges and keep lines well away from propellers. Also, the long, two-fisted handles of popping and flipping rods make for less-strenuous trolling because the rod butts easily can be held with two hands, or the handle can be rested against the angler's knee or boat console for extra support.

Although trolling lipless crankbaits has its origin in Florida, there is no question that trolling the little lures is effective in bass waters everywhere.

Lipless Landing Techniques

The bulletlike design and relatively heavy weight of lipless crankbaits makes it easy for bass to throw these lures. Here are some tips from seminar leader Larry Nixon that will diminish the chances of that happening:

■ Anticipate the jump — When line movement indicates the fish is about to come out of the water, point the rod tip low and pull the fish toward the boat. This usually will prevent the bass from getting its entire body out of the water and helps keep it from shaking its head.

■ Modify the lure to slide up the line — Remove the hooks from a sinking lipless crankbait. Drill a vertical hole through the lure body from close to where the line tie is, straight down. Put a drop or two of cement in the hole and slide a thin plastic tube, like the spray nozzle tube from a can of aerosol lubricant, all the way through, trimming at both ends. Let dry, then run the fishing line through the tube, tie a treble hook to the end and fish the lure like a normal lipless crankbait. When a bass is hooked on the modified crankbait, the heavy lure body slides up the line so the fish can't use it for leverage and throw the hook. Several lure manufacturers offer 'Pro Model' lipless crankbaits factory-rigged for sliding.

■ Modify hooks — Supersharp trebles are ideal for most lipless crankbait applications, but in thick brush or grass, trim the downward hooks off the treble so the lure hangs up less often. Replacing the stock hooks with larger ones can make the lure's vibrations less intense and may trigger more strikes in cold water, but remember that bigger hooks are easier for the bass to throw.

THE ALLURE OF LIPLESS CRANKBAITS

These rattling, vibrating plugs have a knack for calling the biggest bass out of the most obscure hiding places

BILL LEWIS AND COTTON CORDELL couldn't have envisioned what they were starting when they fashioned the first lipless, vibrating crankbaits. Lewis with his Rat-L-Trap and Cordell with his Spot started the lure class that is an integral part of the line-up for more than a dozen national manufacturers today. In the process, lipless crankbaits have become a time-tested, standard tool for the average bass angler. And "Rat-L-Trap fishing" has almost become a generic term for all types of these thin-profile vibrating baits.

How popular are lipless crankbaits these days? So popular that the unmistakable lure is found in the top drawer of most anglers' tackleboxes.

(Opposite page) THE BEAUTY OF fishing with a lipless crankbait is that its retrieve speed can be adjusted to the mood of the fish.

LIPLESS APPEAL

"I think first and foremost, the biggest advantage of a lipless crankbait, like a Cordell Spot, is the amount of water you can cover with the bait in a short amount of time," believes veteran BASS pro Bernie Schultz. "It's effective throughout a variety of depths, from extremely shallow to deep water.

"And lipless crankbaits are one of the high percentage lures in terms of attracting strikes."

The appeal of such hard plastic lures as the Rat-L-Trap and Spot is in the noise they make and the curiosity they create in bass, according to another Florida pro, Shaw Grigsby, who has been a fan of lipless crankbaits since first fishing a Heddon Sonic Perch in the early 1970s. "But don't believe the marketing stuff you hear about such lures making a noise that represents a crawfish. That's all wrong.

"In my opinion, the pure essence of a Rat-L-Trap is that bass are very, very curious. They hear

Crankbait Tip

Use lipless crankbaits that are bright and flashy in clear water on sunny days. Chrome and clear finishes are the most popular choices in these conditions. On cloudy days, flat finishes such as bone and white are most visible to bass and far outfish reflective finishes. In murky water, try hot colors like chartreuse or firetiger.

Lipless By The Season

Follow this seasonal guide to fishing with lipless crankbaits.

■ **Early spring** — In clear, rocky lakes, bass often move up on sunny, unseasonably mild days and hold very shallow around large rocks, where they warm themselves. These bass often can be caught by fishing either a sinking or floating lipless crankbait fairly slowly so it bumps the rocks.

■ **Late spring** — As bass come off their spawning beds, they will feed aggressively — the perfect time for a fast moving lipless crankbait. "Burn" these lures with a fast retrieve in shallow, protected coves and on main lake flats with scattered stumps or patchy weed growth.

■ **Summer** — Large main lake flats will hold active fish, especially those with submerged milfoil, coontail or hydrilla beds. Fish a lipless crankbait quickly with rod held high so it runs just under the surface. Watch for bass chasing schooling baitfish on the surface in open water; a lipless crankbait is a great schooling-bass lure.

■ **Fall** — Bass will be on the move chasing wandering schools of baitfish. Check the mouths of large tributaries. Early and late in the day, fish are likely to be schooling in open water. As the sun gets high, look for them around sheltered areas closer to shore, especially under boat docks. Lipless crankbaits can be used effectively in either scenario.

this lure before it gets to them, and all of a sudden it appears — and they hammer it. This bait calls fish to it because they're very curious."

Grigsby believes that, in most cases, lipless crankbaits represent the size, shape and movements of shad. That makes these crankbaits a prime choice anytime such baitfish are present.

COVERING THE STRUCTURE

As is plain from the following testimonials, practically no type of cover or structure is immune to the effectiveness of lipless crankbaits. But there is one situation where they are most productive.

"They are absolutely at their best in grass lakes, which we consistently prove on the Tournament Trail," Grigsby says. "These lures are outstanding in lakes with hydrilla or milfoil."

Four time world champion Rick Clunn claims they are year-round lures on lakes with vegetation. If weeds are abundant, you can bet he'll have a Rat-L-Trap tied on to a rod and ready for action.

Clunn appreciates the versatility of such lures, particularly their ability to precisely work the contour of weedbeds with just subtle adjustments in rod position. By raising or lowering the rod, he can cause a lipless crankbait to maintain the desired degree of contact with the tops of vegetation.

"These crankbaits are the best baits for what I call 'nonpositional fish' — bass you can't position or pinpoint — which is especially important in fishing grass," Clunn explains. "With weeds, you're mostly fishing blind. You can't predict where these fish are going to come from. These lures call fish to them, so pinpoint positioning isn't crucial."

Clunn cautions that fishing a lipless crankbait around weeds requires patience, since the treble hooks frequently snag in the vegetation. "You've got to put up with a certain amount of frustration," he adds. "The average guy won't tolerate it; he'll either fish outside the weeds or leave. And he will miss out on some prime fishing."

Because they reach the bottom quickly and stay down, Schultz adds, magnum cranks like the 1-ounce Spot are great for working channel bends and edges, humps and even deep grassbeds. Unlike other forms of lipless cranking, probing deep structure involves methodically pumping or retrieving the heavy lures while staying in touch with the bottom.

For the times when the baitfish are small, but positioned around deep structure, Grigsby switches to a 1/2-ounce Rat-L-Trap, which he weights internally with molten lead. This gives him a small-profile crankbait that can be fished like a jigging spoon in 30 feet of water or more.

BEST CASE SCENARIOS

Most bass enthusiasts know just one way to fish a lipless crankbait: fast and steady. But the beauty of these versatile lures lies in their effectiveness in a variety of retrieves.

Arkansas pro Mike Wurm believes there is no wrong way to retrieve the lures. Their

A LIPLESS CRANKBAIT is highly effective in postspawn, when the bass are aggressively feeding.

shadlike shape, attractive noise and motion will draw attention with almost any kind of retrieve.

He recommends experimenting with various speeds and methods. That is how he discovered another excellent application for no-bill crankbaits.

"I use it as a 'drop bait' in late summer, when bass are really becoming active again, chasing shad and starting to migrate back up into the creeks," says Wurm. "In a creek, the bass will follow the shad along ledges and points. Instead of using a topwater bait and waiting for them to school on the surface, I use a lipless crankbait as a drop bait around these deeper migration routes.

"Another good situation to fish lipless crankbaits as drop baits is when the bass come up to school on the surface and then either quit or go down. If I can still see the shad visually or on a depthfinder, I throw the lipless bait into the school of shad and let it sink through them. Bass are almost always following below the bait, and that lure looks like a wounded shad falling right down on them. That's usually too much for them to resist."

SIZING UP WITH COLOR

Like most crankbaits, lipless divers are available in a plethora of sizes and colors. But the truth is, most anglers limit themselves to a few choices.

Grigsby is one of the relatively few fishermen who has incorporated all sizes of lipless crankers into his system of fishing. He fishes the whole Rat-L-Trap lineup from the 1/8-ounce Tiny Trap to the 3/4-ounce Mag-Trap — and has even been experimenting with the whopper 1 1/2-ounce Super-Trap recently.

"Anybody who is fishing just one or two sizes is making a mistake," Grigsby says. "To me, the time of year and size of the bass in a lake determines which size I use."

To most fishermen, any color scheme is fine as long as it involves chrome. Chrome with a blue back is the top selling color for Rat-L-Traps, and black, gold and green-back versions also rank high. But that is changing somewhat, after the recent tournament successes of these lures.

Red, orange and a combination of both have been popular in Texas lakes for some time. In fact, red lipless baits have become known as "Texas baits." But the pros have proved that these are productive colors in any state where aquatic vegetation is abundant.

Grigsby utilizes a variety of color patterns, including those with chrome, red, chartreuse and perch colors. But he works the red-colored versions differently from the others. "I think the red represents a crawfish, and if you've ever spooked a crawfish, you know that they shoot up off the bottom and move pretty quick," Grigsby says. "What you want is an irregular action when the bait hits an object like grass or bushes. To a bass, red represents a crawfish, and that erratic action confirms it."

Lipless Tackle

Pro bass anglers like Larry Nixon prefer long, shock-absorbing cranking rods for lipless crankbaits.

"These lures are very wind resistant and you can cast them a country mile on a two-handed cranking rod," Nixon says. "This is especially important when you're trying to comb a big piece of structure in a hurry, which is a great tournament application for these baits."

Lipless crankbaits are likely to be used shallower, and hence are prone to more bottom contact, than deep diving crankbaits. Therefore, it is especially critical that an abrasion resistant line be used. Braided lines work especially well for lipless styles since depth is not an issue; these lines float and may prohibit diving lures from reaching their maximum depth potential.

BIG, LIPLESS
crankbaits cover
deeper water more
effectively than
heavy jigs and soft
plastics.

GOING DEEP WITH LIPLESS CRANKBAITS

Ready to get your line stretched in deep water? Try these giant plugs for trophy bass

OPEN THE TACKLEBOX of any bass enthusiast in America and chances are great that it will contain at least one lipless crankbait.

When most of these anglers think of lipless crankbaits, their thoughts center around relatively shallow situations like flats, shorelines and grassbeds. With that thought process, they are missing a major point. A deep point, in fact.

Certain top tournament pros have discovered that the larger versions of these flat-sided, noise-making, vibrating plastic lures have a practically unparalleled allure for big bass hanging around deep structure.

"It's probably the best deep water structure bait there is," praises David Fritts, best known for his prowess with big lipped crankbaits. "No bait catches big bass like these baits. None."

It is already well-documented that spinnerbaits, jigs and crankbaits have the ability to attract big

A MAGNUM lipless crankbait will fool a big bass into believing the fake bait is a full meal.

bass. Be sure to add 1-ounce lipless crankbaits to that list, urges Fritts.

When the experts talk about fishing these big, lipless crankbaits around deep structure, they are usually referring to either the 3/4-ounce Rat-L-Trap or Spot — or the 1-ounce grandfather of Cordell baits.

"The 1-ounce Spot is my favorite," says Fritts. "I will fish the 3/4-ounce Rat-L-Trap in a little shallower situation, but it doesn't work as well as that 1-ounce Spot. They make a 1 1/2-ounce 'Trap, but I think it's too big. To fish anything heavier than the 1-ounce Spot means changing to a heavier rod and line, and giving up sensitivity."

Deep structure guru Robert Hamilton prefers the 1-ounce original Spot over its 3/4-ounce competitor for structure 15 feet and deeper. Regardless of how slowly the Rat-L-Trap is worked, it has a tendency to rise and lose contact with the bottom, he says.

According to the pros, there is plenty to like about these monstrous plugs.

Among the qualities that make them such prime and underrated trophy bass lures are these:

• Quick and slow — Big, lipless crankbaits permit covering deep water fast and effectively much faster than can be accomplished with soft plastics, says Fritts. What's more, it has good action while being moved slowly, which enables it to attract bigger bass. "It's like slow rolling a big spinnerbait," he suggests. "You don't get many bites, but they're usually big fish. Only, you can fish this bait faster than a spinnerbait, because it's so heavy and it drops like a rock."

• Bottom detection — With so much weight,

these lures can decipher the layout of the bottom, including its composition and the location of any submerged object.

• Depth-defying — Lipless crankbaits can be worked at almost any depth, Fritts adds. "You're limited to just fishing a foot or so off the bottom. I like to rip it 3 or 4 feet off the bottom, so it covers more area."

• Sheer size — Big lures attract bigger bass, the pros emphasize. And big, lipless cranks are just right for southern lakes, and others with populations of big gizzard shad.

• Seductive sound — BASS superstar Kevin VanDam says the unique sound of the big Spot will trigger strikes from bass that have ignored other lures. Hamilton agrees, but notes that the original Spot has a single rattle, while the newer version has BBs that give it a higher-pitched, faster sound — more like that of a Rat-L-Trap. "And there are days when they will bite one and not the other," he has found.

Hamilton calls them "mop-up baits," while VanDam prefers the term "backup lure." Both emphasize that they are excellent tools for following behind more conventional deep structure lures, like diving crankbaits and slow rolled spinnerbaits, for bass that aren't biting or have suddenly stopped cooperating.

Crankbait Tip

When combing shallow water with a lipless crankbait, keep the rod higher than when fishing with deep divers. Lipless crankbaits can hang up repeatedly if the angler tries to bump them off cover. Long rods are helpful not only for their shock absorption, but because they may be used to steer the lure around scattered, shallow objects.

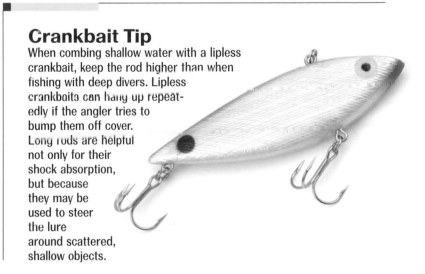

Traits Of Lipless Crankbaits

■ **Lure color** — Throughout the year, David Fritts limits his choices to a shad color with either a black or blue back. Robert Hamilton relies on chrome, shad and chartreuse, depending on water clarity. VanDam likes shad, pearl white and chartreuse, but he also scores impressively with red and crawfish patterns in the grass laden lakes of the South.

■ **Hooking problems** — Smaller, lipless crankbaits are notorious for being dislodged during a fight. The problem is the weight of these flat-bodied lures, which can be used as leverage to free a treble hook. The problem is even more severe with these huge baits.

"The heavier the bait, the more chance the bass has to throw it," Hamilton says. "But there are a couple of things you can do. If you can get past the initial jump, you can usually land the fish. So if you feel the fish coming up, stick your rod down in the water and put a little pressure on it. If the fish doesn't jump, try to keep pressure on it and pull it back down."

Hamilton also improves his chances by adding a small Sampo ball-bearing swivel between the rear hook and its holder. The swivel enables the lure to spin, and minimizes

leverage from its weight. The back hook is the only one that is modified this way, because it is the most likely hook to snag a bass.

■ **Getting unhung** — These bulky lures will inevitably get hung up, so Fritts keeps a Gripper Lure Retriever (his own design) nearby. He offers a valuable tip: "The key is not to jerk on the bait real hard when it gets hung. Get right over the top of it and wiggle it straight up and down. If you don't jerk too hard, the weight of the bait sometimes works the hooks free."

THE PROS sometimes use lipless crankbaits as backup lures when they know fish are present and will not hit the first offering.

"I always throw that big bait before I leave a hole," says Hamilton, who has caught largemouth as deep as 25 feet with the 3/4-ounce Rat-L-Trap and 1-ounce Spot.

A major reason for the success of oversize lipless lures is that they reach bass at levels other baits barely approach.

"To me, it complements a crankbait like a Poe's," Fritts explains. "When you get beyond the effective range of a crankbait — 20 feet or so — a crankbait loses more fish than it catches. That's where these big baits kick in. They're superb for 20 feet deep and deeper."

Fritts' other deep water mainstay, the Carolina rig, is effective below 20 feet, but it's a slow working bait compared to a big Spot or Rat-L-Trap.

Although these magnum plugs will catch quality bass throughout the year, certain times find them much more productive than others.

They really shine from postspawn through summer, Fritts and VanDam agree. Anytime bass are dormant, from the stifling heat of summer to the frigid spells of winter, Fritts can be found probing the depths with big Rat-L-Traps or original Spots. In winter, on lakes like Wylie on the border of the two Carolinas, a boss lipless crankbait will outproduce the more traditional

jigging spoon when worked vertically along river channel edges and the intersection of any two channels, he claims.

GEARING UP

These enormous baits demand strong, balanced tackle.

Hamilton and Fritts stress that stout, 7 1/2-foot fiberglass rods are best-suited for the strain and strategies of the technique. The strength of fiberglass enables the angler to rip these lures sharply off the bottom, and because fiberglass is more "forgiving," it gives the angler an edge in keeping big bass from throwing treble hooks. Although not as sensitive as graphite, glass rods have enough sensitivity to detect the vibrations of the lure.

Line is a major consideration. Although none of our experts rely on braided line much, this is a situation where a low stretch superline, like SpiderWire Fusion, combined with a fiberglass rod can actually provide more sensitivity than graphite and monofilament, according to Hamilton.

All three have different philosophies about line size. Fritts relies on 17- to 25-pound-test Stren. VanDam drops to 10- or 12-pound Trilene XT, claiming heavier line hampers his ability to keep the big lure in contact with the bottom. Although he allows water clarity to dictate line size, Hamilton primarily uses 14- to 17-pound green Trilene XT.

WORKING THE GIANT

"There are several ways you can fish these baits," Hamilton emphasizes. "You have a choice of casting them out or vertically jigging them. You can slow roll them like you would a big spinnerbait, letting them bang around along the bottom."

He enjoys his best luck by picking the bait up and letting it fall. "I cast it out and let it hit bottom, then really rip it 6 to 8 feet off the bottom," he says. "I think one of the keys to this bait is fishing it a little faster and more erratically than you would a regular crankbait."

A deadly retrieve in Fritts' arsenal involves casting the lure out, turning the reel handle six or seven times with the rod tip at the 1 o'clock position, then pausing to allow it to sink. This causes the lure to fall back toward the boat instead of straight down — an action that often creates strikes.

"If I'm fishing deep structure with hard bottoms, I like to jig or pump the bait, which allows me to cover more of the depth zones there," VanDam advises. "Cover like grass or brush requires a totally different approach. The first step is to try to visualize the area and what it has to offer in the way of cover. With its weight and two treble hooks, this bait is more prone to hang up than a lipped crankbait, so it's better for catching bass that are not real tight to the cover."

A LIPLESS crankbait imitates a shad, the forage favored by bass in the fall, when cooling water triggers their appetite.

FALLING FOR LIPLESS CRANKBAITS

Just find a shallow flat loaded with baitfish and seine it with a lipless crankbait

EVERY AUTUMN, Arkansas angler Mark Rose is torn between two passions — bass fishing and deer hunting. Even when he pulls a boat to BASS Tour events, a compound bow sometimes comes along for the ride.

Rose literally wears his dilemma on the camouflaged sleeves of his tournament shirt. It is also evident on his camouflaged tow vehicle and bass boat.

What makes Rose's fix so perplexing is that just about the time cool fall weather puts whitetail bucks on the prowl, bass swarm shallow flats where they readily succumb to Rose's rattling lipless crankbaits. Does he head for the woods or the water?

"It really isn't much of a problem," says Rose. "The best fishing on flats usually takes place in the middle of the day, especially when the sun shines. I can hunt in the morning and still have plenty of time to load up on bass."

While it's common knowledge that bass follow shad into the shallows when temperatures cool in the fall, few anglers probe the paper-thin water that Rose seines with rattling crankbaits. He trims his outboard above the waterline, raises the electric motor so high the prop's blade sometimes sputters the surface, and nudges his boat ever shallower, kicking up a trail of silt as he goes. Most of his bass come from water less than 2 feet deep; some less than 12 inches deep.

"Some of my best catches have come in water so shallow, you think you would see the bass," says Rose.

Rose learned the intricacies of fishing flats on his home water, the Mississippi River. This pattern has come through for him many times on impoundments and river systems across the country from October through December. He claims flats sometimes pay off during warm fronts in midwinter, as well. Bass start feeding actively on flats, Rose has found, when the water temperature drops to the mid-70s.

"When the water cools on those flats," says Rose, "bass work together like a pack of wolves and pen up the shad. Their instincts tell them cold weather is coming, and they're feeding while they can."

The most productive flats contain stained water and a creek channel or ditch that bass use as a migration route into the shallows. A depression 3 to 4 feet deep that bisects a flat 1 to 2 feet deep is all it takes. These subtle pathways also give Rose's boat avenues from which to navigate flats.

Stained water with a visibility of less than 12 inches is crucial. When Rose faces clear water or mocha mud, he eschews flats in favor of other patterns. Productive flats are typically located in the backwaters of large river systems and the upriver sections of impoundments. But Rose doesn't overlook the lower reaches of impoundments in his search for skinny bass water. He frequently finds flats with stained water in the very backs of pockets off the main lake.

If Rose finds an expansive flat thick with baitfish and bass, he may stay put and rework the area several times over the course of the day. In most instances, however, he bounces from one flat to another, covering six to eight of them in a milk run that keeps a serious bend in his rod. Given stable weather and water conditions, the same flats yield bass day after day.

"If the body of water you are fishing has one productive flat, it usually has several others," says Rose. "I fan cast one flat thoroughly and move on. You cover a lot of water fast this way. It's so efficient."

When searching for bass, Rose's spirits soar whenever he sees abundant shad activity on the surface of a flat. If shad are present, he reasons, bass will move in to feed on them. Then again, flats with little baitfish activity have also given up good bass for Rose, so he doesn't automatically write them off. A reconnaissance with a rattle bait makes the final determination. In some instances, a flat will appear lifeless early in the

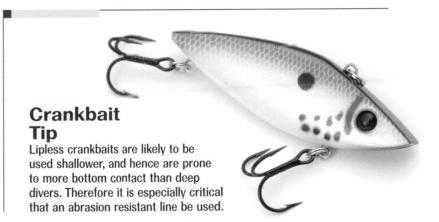

Crankbait Tip

Lipless crankbaits are likely to be used shallower, and hence are prone to more bottom contact than deep divers. Therefore it is especially critical that an abrasion resistant line be used.

Lipless Crankbaits In Grass

Several BASS tournaments have been won by pros using lipless crankbaits in submerged grassbeds. Here's how to do it:

Locate likely grassbeds for cranking — Not all grassbeds are conducive to fishing with lipless crankbaits. Those that are tend to hold active fish; watch for baitfish movement on top of and at the outer perimeter of the bed.

Burn the grassline — On a weedbed with a well-defined outer edge or "grassline," active bass will cruise the edge, taking advantage of forage species holding both in the grass and in open water. Position the boat so casts can be made parallel to the grassline; retrieve the lipless crankbait quickly and very close to the grass.

Tick the top — Where weeds top out just below the surface, active fish often will cruise the top of the bed, looking for bluegills or shiners. A fast moving lipless crankbait often triggers strikes in such circumstances. If the lure consistently fouls in the grass, switch to a floating model or try a buzzbait or soft jerkbait instead.

Bump and jump — Deep, isolated hydrilla or coontail beds are sometimes the key to huge concentrations of big bass. Deep diving crankbaits are impossible to fish through this grass; jigs and worms are better but may be too slow for tournament use. Try a sinking lipless crankbait instead. Note the depth of the weedbed on the fishfinder. Cast to the bed, let the lure sink on a tight line and count the lure down to just above the level of the grass, then snap the rod tip. The lure will dart and flash, looking much like a frightened baitfish.

morning or during cloudy weather, but come alive when warm sunshine revitalizes shad and draws them to the surface.

"The absolute best-case scenario," says Rose, "is stained water, high sun, baitfish and a water temperature in the high 60s. You can catch them under cloudy conditions, but the fishing is best under the midday sun."

When fishing flats, he generally has the water pretty much to himself. Yes, many anglers fish shallow water in the fall, but few are willing to plow silt as Rose does. And when the sun gets high, which is when flat fishing peaks, many of Rose's competitors elect to fish a little deeper.

"When most people start fishing deeper, I'm trying to get my boat as shallow as it will go," says Rose.

One word of warning, however. Cold, cloudy days, especially when accompanied by chilly rain, can turn bass off and push them to even deeper water. As always, it pays to have backup patterns.

Many flats that have produced big catches for Rose offer little in the way of cover. He targets snags, sparse grass and even twigs sticking up through the surface whenever he sees such objects, but he's really not concerned with the presence of cover. It simply isn't necessary to catch bass.

A LIPLESS crankbait can provide fast, productive action in fall, when bass herd shad onto shallow flats adjacent to deep water.

Lipless Crankbaits For Schooling Bass

Relatively few anglers fish lipless crankbaits for bass "in the jumps," but they're unusually effective for this application. Here's how the pros do it:

Keep your distance — Schooling bass are spooky; they'll dive back down if they sense an intruder. Lipless crankbaits are perfect for surfacing fish since they can be cast extremely long distances and have the flash of live shad.

Burn it — Make a long cast and "burn" the lure so it runs just under the surface. Often a bass — sometimes two — will nail it immediately.

Drop it — If the bass won't strike, or only small bass will strike when the lure is retrieved near the surface, cast, retrieve the bait close to the top for a few feet, then stop reeling and let it fall on a tight line. Often bigger bass are holding beneath the smaller "schoolies," feeding on injured shad that drift downward.

Rose nets fish from what looks to be barren water with a Strike King Diamond Shad lipless rattling crankbait. He fares best with the 1/4-ounce size in black and blue, and black and gold. Before he fishes a Diamond Shad, he scrapes the shiny metallic paint off the lower half of the bait with a knife or the sharp edge of a pair of scissors. This reveals a dull, bone-gray plastic, which tones down the flash and gives the lure a more realistic appearance.

Rose slings the Diamond Shad on 15-pound P-Line with a 6-foot, 6-inch, G. Loomis medium action baitcasting rod and a Shimano Chronarch reel with a 6.2:1 gear ratio.

"I reel the bait along just fast enough so it is barely making bottom contact," says Rose. "I don't lift and drop the bait or give it any kind of action with my reel. I want a steady retrieve that kicks up silt. I'm not burning the bait, but I'm not working it slow, either."

In water less than 1 foot deep, Rose holds the rod tip high to keep the Diamond Shad working properly. In 2 to 4 feet of water, he lowers his rod tip. The high speed reel helps him maintain control over the retrieve and keep pressure on bass after they pounce on his bait.

"A lot of times, bass run straight at you when they hit," says Rose. "That's because your boat is in slightly deeper water, and that's where they want to go. A high speed reel helps you catch up to them. Set your drag light. This pattern produces big bass."

ALL ABOUT JERKBAITS

How To Use The Most
Versatile And Effective
Reaction Bait …

WHEN TO STICK WITH JERKBAITS

Follow these lessons for year-round jerking

IT WOULD NOT BE stretching the truth very far to say that jerkbaits are year-round lures. Granted, their use in the dead of winter or the dog days of summer may be questioned, but having a few on hand at all times is not a bad idea. An even better idea is learning when jerkbaits are at their very best.

For Mark Menendez, the jerkbait has been a crucial tool in his professional career, one that has helped produce multiple Bassmaster Classic ap-

pearances and a Tour victory at Alabama's Pickwick Lake.

Ask him when his thoughts turn to these darting, dancing lures, and the Kentucky pro will quickly reel off three key periods: prespawn, postspawn and fall.

PRESPAWN

"In the prespawn, you know the backs of the creeks are out. You know the quantity of fish just

isn't back there. This alone cuts down your search.

"As a result, you should focus your efforts in the front one-third of the bay and be looking at primary and secondary points."

In particular, Menendez is looking for short, flat points that offer immediate deep water access. Since this early spring attack is centered on bass that are not relating to the bottom, the presence of bait is an indicator of those areas where fish are actively suspending.

The contact zone on these areas — the place where the fish move up and down on the structure — is where the point flattens out and then immediately drops off into deeper water.

With frigid water temperatures from 42 to 50 degrees, the fish do not stay in these contact zones very long, notes Menendez, because their metabolism is slow, and they don't need to feed that often. Generally, they move up briefly to forage and then slide back into deeper water. As a result, the success of early season jerkbaiting often depends on being at the right place at the right time.

"You have two bites. You have an early morning bite every day from when the sun comes up until about 9 or 10 o'clock. Then it stirs up again later in the afternoon, as the wind picks up between 2 and 5 p.m. The wind activates the environment and puts the bass in that predator mode."

Moreover, this timing scenario helps prevent even obvious spots from getting pounded, since many anglers are not diligent enough to stay on the bite. The other factor that separates the fish catchers from everyone else is the jerking cadence itself.

"Many anglers fish too fast, jerk too hard and don't wait long enough between pauses. This time of year, you need to tap that bait so it gets off-center; so it makes a very slight little flutter. It shouldn't move forward very far most of the time in that cold water."

During the prespawn, Menendez generally relies on 8-pound test and one of his signature series suspending Smithwick Rogues, because of its subtle action and tendency to roll up on its side and flash when twitched.

POSTSPAWN

As the season moves closer to summer and the females are pulling off the beds, Menendez again gears up his jerkbait assault by targeting the back one-third of the bays.

"Seeing fry is the key. Most of the first spawning pockets are located on the northeast side of a lake. So, I'm looking at those pockets and the secondary points leading from those pockets.

"The real cool little places are small pockets with a nice slope. And you can go back in those pockets to see where they actually flatten out. They're roaming between there and the actual point of the pocket.

"Actually, they're pretty easy to figure out. If you start on the main part of the point, work your way back and catch them out in front, you stay out there."

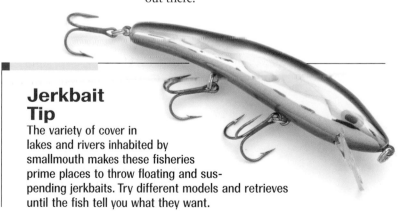

Jerkbait Tip
The variety of cover in lakes and rivers inhabited by smallmouth makes these fisheries prime places to throw floating and suspending jerkbaits. Try different models and retrieves until the fish tell you what they want.

The Pause For The Cause

Even if a jerkbait fisherman tells you the cadence he's using to catch bass, it isn't enough information. It's more than knowing how to jerk the bait, says Mark Menendez, but also how to pause it.

Of the two things a jerkbait fisherman needs to know — how hard to jerk and how long to pause — the pause is the key. While there are no hard-and-fast rules, water temperature is generally the best guideline. In colder water, lengthen the pauses and snap the bait less sharply.

"If they're eating it on the tail treble, you definitely need to pause longer. They're looking at the bait for a long time before making up their minds," observes Menendez. "If they're eating it at the head or midsection, you've got it figured out."

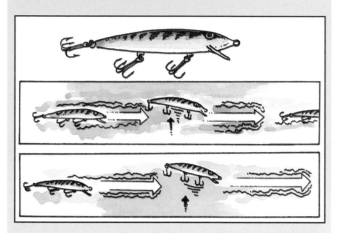

JERKBAITS ARE effective lures for fishing bare banks because they attract bass from a distance.

This strategy can pay even bigger dividends on lakes with an abundance of docks, since most anglers will key on these obvious targets and leave the open pockets between them virtually untouched. By keying on these "nothing banks" — places with a gentle slope and hard bottom — says Menendez, a fisherman can intercept bass that are "roaming out there because they're hungry and ready to eat something.

"What you end up doing is finding them in a particular depth zone. Generally, I end up wanting to have my boat in 5 to 7 feet of water and fishing in 2 to 5 feet.

"But this is often a temporary deal, a two to four week thing at the most. Fish can move from day to day, so it's probably a better recreational pattern than a tournament pattern."

In warmer, postspawn water, Menendez shifts to 14-pound test and a Bomber Long A, a jerkbait with a wider side-to-side action.

FALL

As shad begin their migration back into the creeks (generally a late September to early October phenomenon), Menendez shifts his focus to creek channels. These submerged highways make this a somewhat more dependable bite than postspawn, because an angler has a more direct route to stay with the fish.

Jerkbait Tactics For River Smallmouth

Smallmouth that live in free-flowing rivers are just as eager to slam a jerkbait as are their lake-bound relatives. Ralph Capasso, a guide on the upper Potomac and Susquehanna rivers, uses hard jerkbaits nearly all year.

"Jerkbaits tend to work best in clear water, but if it's a little stained, I'll just use something like a firetiger or clown Rattlin' Rogue," he says. "I've caught smallmouth on them starting in February, when the water is in the low 40s right through late fall, when the water drops back down into the 40s. There really is no wrong time to use them."

Although Capasso describes himself as a die-hard fan of tube jigs, he had an exceptional day with jerkbaits one recent February day on the upper Potomac River that affirmed his belief in hard jerkbaits. After searching for bass in the warmwater discharge of a coal-fired power plant, he abandoned the 55 degree water and went to the opposite shore, where the water was a chilly 42 degrees. In about four hours, Capasso caught 22 small-

mouth, including five that totaled 24 pounds.

"The water was clearer on that side of the river, but I wasn't really expecting to catch much in the colder water, which was only 100 yards away from the warmer water. But it sure worked that day," he recalls.

Instead of fishing the Rogue with the standard jerk-pause, jerk-pause retrieve, Capasso was simply swimming the lure back to the boat. Most of the time, however, he does use the usual retrieve all bass anglers associate with jerkbaits.

"A real neat thing to do is use them almost like a topwater. I'll throw a floating Long A out and just let it sit still for 10 or 15 seconds. I might twitch it a few times, but I usually don't need to," he says. "That technique works best if there is a slight breeze. Otherwise, I'll jerk it under and let it float up."

Earlier in the season, when the water temp is in the 50s and low 60s, Capasso uses a suspending jerkbait around typical current breaks such as midriver boulders, grassbeds and islands.

"While they may get off that creek channel and chase the bait around, they will come back to it. I really like finding a creek channel with the bottom in 10 feet and the sides in 5 feet or less. I will go up that creek channel just as if I had a crankbait tied on, fan casting off into the flats, reeling it out to the deep. That's generally when you get your bites.

"Since I need to snap it and really make an impression, I prefer to use 12-pound test and a Bomber Long A with a lot of flash to it."

However, regardless of the season, choosing the right rod for jerkbaits is of paramount concern. Although casting accuracy is a consideration, the cushioning aspect of the rod plays an even greater role, counsels Menendez, who uses a 6-6 medium action Pflueger Trion.

"The jerkbait rods I've used over the last 10 years all had one thing in common: They were 6-6 and more parabolic, like a crankbait rod. I tend to use one that is somewhat lighter than the norm, because you're dealing with so many treble hooks. If fish bite the back hook, you have to be careful. When the bass surges, the rod needs to bend. A rod like this won't work you as hard when you're throwing it day in and day out.

"In the prespawn, it's all about angles. All you have to do is set up the angle.

"In the postspawn, sling it down the bank, hurry up and go. In the fall, you may be around schooling fish, so you do need a little more accuracy."

BECAUSE THE bass can strike a jerkbait with force, the experts prefer parabolic rods — for their forgiving action.

THE SUSPENDING JERKBAIT ZONE

Use this specialized approach in clear, cold water

WHETHER IT'S A MOVIE or a fishing lure, the sequel is rarely as good as the original. At least, that's the case most of the time. There are, however, some noteworthy exceptions to the rule, and one of the most beneficial for bass fishermen has been the suspending jerkbait.

Long before lure manufacturers figured out how to make these baits suspend and perform, anglers had proved the consistent, fish-catching ability of the floating versions. By the time suspending models were introduced, bass fishermen were well-schooled on jerkbait techniques and saw the potential in neutrally buoyant baits.

"The most common time we think of suspending jerkbaits is very early in the spring (prespawn) when the water is clear and cold. The fish are slow to react because they're lethargic. The water is warming a little, but it's still pretty cold — in the 40s and low 50s," counsels Ken Cook, a former fisheries biologist-turned BASS pro.

"A suspending bait gets down to

Jerkbait Tip
Because it is a "sight" lure, a weighted jerkbait works best in clear water that has a visibility of 3 feet or more. It will catch fish throughout the year, but is more effective in the spring.

the zone, or near the zone, where they're holding. In these conditions, the fish tend to suspend a lot. It seems as though the sharp jerking action wakes them up and pushes their buttons. It creates a hard thump and makes a sudden motion that tends to wake up their reactions. Then, it just stays there. This is why the suspending action is so important."

Summer and fall also afford excellent opportunities for suspending jerkbaits, particularly in those situations when bass are positioned in slightly deeper water. Although Cook typically

fishes the baits much faster during the warmer seasons — shortening the pauses between jerks as well — the basic elements necessary for success still apply.

Cook's outline of those requirements follows:

• You need clear water — 2 feet or better visibility.

• You need the fish to react, whether the result of a sudden impulse or a slow building curiosity.

• You don't need baitfish.

• Ideally, you would like some targets or edge cover from which to pull fish.

Even though most suspending jerkbaits come equipped with a rattling mechanism, the ultimate triggering system here is largely dependent on the visual component. The darts, flashes, stops and starts are what "sells" the bait to the fish.

For each angler, this blank canvas allows every retrieve to be personalized. With action and depth control that far surpasses most other hard baits, fishermen are not limited by the lure itself. In essence, they can separate themselves from every other angler on the water by creating a bite that may not exist for anyone else.

Jerkbaits By The Dot

Even though suspending jerkbaits are designed to suspend right out of the box, not all perform equally well. In most cases, Ken Cook wants his lure to suspend horizontally. If he needs to adjust how the lure sits in the water, he first finds the exact balance point of the bait. To do so, he loops a short piece of monofilament around the lure and weights it with a small sinker. In a sink filled with water, this rig will pull the bait down just enough to find the critical center point.

To adjust the balance, he adds Storm SuspendDots. If dots are placed incorrectly, they can be peeled off and reattached to fine-tune the process.

"If I nose-weight the lure just a little, I get more depth out of the bait. For a nose-down rig, I'll put spots on the back of the bill, out of the water flow.

"Closer to the spawning season, I'll add extra weight so it will sink slowly, again nose-down (at approximately 30 degrees). This is very intimidating to a bass around a bed."

"Most people just aren't willing to work at it hard enough," advises Cook.

"First, you have to read the timing of the fish. That is, the timing and type of jerking action the fish want. You want to figure out how long you need between jerks, how many and how quick the motion should be. This is what you do when you're first trying to develop a pattern."

Keeping a close eye on water temperature is one way Cook tries to make some sense of how the fish want the lure presented. But rather than keying on specific temperature ranges, he is far more concerned with an in-water temperature.

"Say the water is relatively cold and a cold front is moving through. If it's cloudy and the cold front hasn't come through yet, there will probably be more active fish. If the cold front went through yesterday, the water temperature has dropped a few degrees, the sun is high and bright and the fish are less active, I'll start off slower."

With clear water, the right conditions and a good pair of polarized sunglasses, it is often possible to actually see bass strike the lure. This is a huge advantage in several respects.

First, if you can see the bass, you can see the bait. As a result, an angler has a much better idea of what the lure was doing at the precise moment of the strike. This is why it is so crucial for fishermen to spend some practice time in a pool or clear water environment learning the peculiarities of a lure. Not all jerkbaits are created equal, and most have some well-defined strengths and weaknesses when it comes to presentation.

How much input does it take to produce a desired response? Does the lure work well at ultraslow speeds? There are a thousand questions that can be answered.

Second, even if you only see the flash of a bass as it streaks toward the lure, you've learned something. You've seen where it came from, how far it moved to get the lure and how fast it responded. There is enough data in that one moment to make some reasonably sound decisions on speed, cadence and casting angles.

However, none of this means a thing if an angler is not disciplined enough to remember exactly what was going on when the bass struck the lure. Was the bait stopped? Did the fish hit immediately after two or three quick jerks? What happened?

Using jerkbaits in the search mode places even greater importance on being able to assess and then duplicate every cast. Since each presentation could possibly result in a

Short Strike Solutions

It's not unusual for smallmouth to follow a jerkbait all the way back to the boat without striking the lure. In fact, it's frustratingly common. Bass will nip at the lure as it darts through the water, but they just won't commit to making a meal out of it. Alabama BASS pro and jerkbait expert Tim Horton says the most important aspect of curing short strikes is knowing that bass are actually doing it.

"I think a lot of times, guys don't even realize that fish are following their baits. That's why it's so important to use a quality pair of polarized sunglasses. I'm a huge fan of Action Optics sunglasses. Not only can you see the make-up of the bottom, you can see how the fish are reacting to your lure," explains Horton. "Are they hanging back and just following the bait? Or are they actually rushing it each time you jerk it? Those are questions you have to answer."

It's fairly common for smallmouth in lakes and rivers to rush a Rogue, only to swipe at the lure or nip at the tail, missing the hooks completely. When that happens, Horton tries a slight adjustment. Sometimes, a simple change in lure color or retrieve speed will make a difference. Moving the lure faster will give the appearance of a frightened baitfish, and that can excite the bass into actually eating your jerkbait. Even a change in direction, which can be accomplished by shifting the angle of your rod tip, can trigger an indecisive bass into striking your lure.

"I like to keep a follow-up bait, like a floating Riverside Jitter Worm, handy. If a smallmouth follows my Rogue back to the boat, it will often hit a floating worm if I just let it fall slowly," notes Horton. "A lot of times, they see the boat, swim away and then turn and look back. Those are the fish that will hit a follow-up bait."

strike, suspending jerkbaits require an inordinate degree of concentration.

Although suspending jerkbaits can be worked as quickly as spinnerbaits or crankbaits, admits Cook, they are still very effective in covering water. This is especially true in coldwater conditions when, as Cook points out, "you can't fish anything all that fast and still expect to catch fish."

In terms of tackle considerations, Cook uses a rod that is somewhat shorter than might be expected. To help maintain a rod position with the tip pointed at the water, his 6-2 Berkley Lightning rod provides just the right length. However, the optimum rod length will change from angler to angler, depending on their stature.

"You need a rod short enough so you can fish it with the rod tip down. You want your line perpendicular to the rod so you can get the most out of your retrieve. It needs to be a fairly light-tipped rod, and it can't be too stiff or totally limp, because you need to impart that jerking motion to the bait."

KEEP A CLOSE eye on changes in water temperature to determine jerkbait presentation.

WINDY CONDITIONS push baitfish against rocky banks, like bluffs. As a result, a jerkbait can be worked at the level where the fish and bait are suspending.

JERKBAITS, ROCKS AND GRASS

Regardless of the cover type, hard minnow plugs
— especially suspending versions —
are hard to beat in clear, cold water

NOW THAT JERKBAITS have become established as essential bass lures, a consensus exists among many respected anglers regarding when and where to cast these baits for optimal success.

Since a bass responds to a jerkbait mainly through its sense of sight, clear water ensures more strikes. A visibility of 2 feet is minimal, and some accomplished anglers won't cast a jerkbait unless visibility exceeds 3 feet.

As for primary jerkbait cover, rocks and aquatic vegetation stand apart from other options. In early spring, main lake bluff walls figure high on Tim Horton's jerkbait hit list. The highly successful Alabama BASS pro claims he fishes jerkbaits as much as 70 percent of the time during the prespawn phase.

BLUFF WALLS

"The best time to fish rocky bluffs is when the water temperature climbs to the high 40s to low 50s," says Horton. "That's when you'll catch big females feeding up before they move into spawning areas. This pattern works on Pickwick, Wilson, Ouachita, Lake of the Ozarks, Bull Shoals and many other clear water impoundments."

Horton concentrates his casts on bluffs where the walls start to break up, where points form and where the rock composition changes.

(Opposite page) IN CLEAR WATER, bass can see a jerkbait above them, tricking them into striking the bait sooner than they would hit a crankbait running below or past them.

While searching for bass along bluffs with a depthfinder, Horton often finds them suspended about 15 feet deep over 20 or more feet of water. McCoy Mean Green 8-pound copolymer allows Horton

Jerkbait Tip
It's not unusual for smallmouth to follow a jerkbait all the way back to the boat without striking the lure. Sometimes, a simple change in lure color or retrieve speed will make a difference. Moving the lure faster will give the appearance of a frightened baitfish, and can excite the bass into eating the lure.

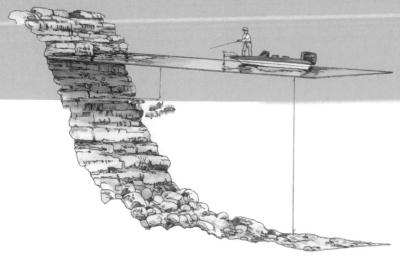

to work a 5-inch suspending Super Rogue 6 to 7 feet deep and to impart a livelier action than can be accomplished with heavier line.

"Early in the spring, I have more success drawing bass up to a jerkbait than running a crankbait down past them," says Horton. "When they see a jerkbait above them, I think bass commit to the strike before they get a close look at the bait."

Horton flings a clown-color Rogue most often, and he frequently does well with a chrome Rogue sporting a black back and orange belly. He casts these lures with a 6-foot, 6-inch Pflueger Trion medium heavy graphite baitcasting rod. The exception is when he is bucking a stiff wind, in which case he switches to a spinning rod in the same length and action to avoid backlashes and achieve sufficient casting distance.

To stay in tune with bass, Horton's jerkbait cadence varies considerably. He typically gives the bait two or three jerks between pauses. The length of the pause may be as long as 15 seconds in cold water, or just a heartbeat after the water warms and bass are more active. As a general rule, he employs a more upbeat retrieve when fishing for smallmouth and spots than when fishing for largemouth.

GRASS BASS

Prespawn bass also swarm aquatic vegetation, such as hydrilla and milfoil. No one is more aware of this fact than Ohio BASS veteran Joe Thomas, who relies heavily on jerkbaits when fishing such grass-rich impoundments as Sam Rayburn and Guntersville. Thomas begins catching bass from grass on jerkbaits when the water hits 50 degrees, and he continues to have success with this approach until the bass commence spawning.

"Early in the spring, I concentrate on emerging grass near secondary points in coves," says Thomas. "There may not be any grass on the point itself, because it may have a hard bottom, such as gravel. The grass usually grows in pockets adjacent to the points. The bass may stage on the points first, and then move into the grass to feed before they spawn."

If Thomas finds grass growing about 18 inches tall in 4 to 7 feet of water around a secondary point, his pulse quickens. He regards this as a superb combination for prespawn jerkbait fishing. The grass is too short to be seen with the eye and must be located with a depthfinder.

"When the grass is short, you may not find a well-defined edge," says Thomas. "That's really not a big deal, because the bass could be anywhere in the grassbed."

Thomas keeps his boat moving while he fan casts a Lucky Craft Pointer 100 or Staysee jerkbait over the grass. The short-billed Pointer 100 runs 3 to 4 feet deep on the 12-pound Stren Moss Green monofilament Thomas always uses when fishing jerkbaits over grass. The long-billed Staysee digs to about 6 feet. Thomas

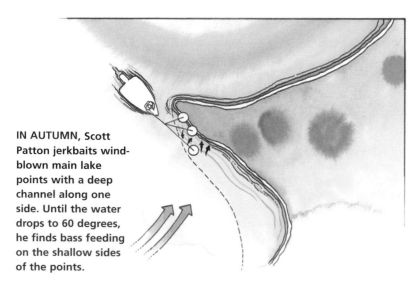

IN AUTUMN, Scott Patton jerkbaits wind-blown main lake points with a deep channel along one side. Until the water drops to 60 degrees, he finds bass feeding on the shallow sides of the points.

GIVE A JERKBAIT two or three tugs between pauses and make the pause longer — up to 15 seconds — in cold water, when the bass are lethargic.

goes with whichever model is required to occasionally snatch the tips of the grass.

"I snap the jerkbait slowly across the grass with a *jerk-jerk, pause; jerk-jerk, pause,*" says Thomas. "The only thing I change is the length of the pauses. When the water's 50 degrees, I might give the pause a three count, which seems like an eternity when you're fishing in a tournament."

"When you find an opening like that in a grassbed, you'll usually catch numerous fish," says Thomas. "I do get big fish on this pattern, but I have better luck catching limits of keeper bass with it."

As the water warms in the spring, the grass grows closer to the surface as bass move farther back into more protected waters, where they eventually spawn. At this time, the grass is plainly visible beneath the surface through polarized sunglasses.

If the shallow bottom has clumps of grass with sandy bare spots in it, Thomas knows he has found ideal jerkbait water. He casts his bait beyond individual grass clumps and twitches it past the cover. Because the water is generally out of the wind, the bass often respond to a more subtle presentation. Thomas adjusts by switching to a 3-inch Pointer 78, which runs 2 to 3 feet deep.

Weather and water conditions dictate Thomas' jerkbait color. In cold water, he favors Lucky Craft's Nishiki (clown). He responds to bright skies with Aurora Black, which has a black back, bluish silver sides and a white belly. Under cloudy conditions, he favors gold with a black back and orange belly.

AUTUMN ROCKS

Jerkbait fishing picks up again in the fall, as cooling water pulls shad and other baitfish up from deep water. The baitfish often congregate on riprap, and chunk rock on which algae has grown. Windy conditions also push baitfish against rocky banks. Bass follow their food source, which allows Kentuckian Scott Patton to pick them off the rocks with a 5 1/2-inch Rapala Husky Jerk.

Fishing a jerkbait in autumn produces largemouth and smallmouth bass for Patton. "The action starts picking up in October. I find a lot of bass on secondary points in creeks. I have good luck on points made up of riprap or natural rock."

The most productive points, Patton has found, have a channel with deeper water that swings close to them. Early in the fall, he concentrates on points in the midsections of major creek arms. As the water continues to cool, Patton finds bass on secondary points farther up into the creeks. The points are likely to yield bass anytime in autumn, but they are at their best when a stiff wind blows.

"When the wind drives baitfish tight to the rocks, I keep my boat close to the bank and work a jerkbait parallel to the point," says Patton. "I try to keep my bait in water from about 2 to 10 feet deep."

Patton also fishes windblown main lake points with his jerkbaits, especially points that have a deep channel running along one side. Many anglers overlook bass in these locations because they concentrate on the steep side of the point, where the bottom plunges to 30 feet or more. Before the water temperature drops below 60 degrees or so, Patton finds bass feeding on the shallow sides of such points.

Please Leave Me Hanging

Tim Horton, Joe Thomas and Scott Patton prefer suspending jerkbaits to floaters. Suspending models run deeper and hover enticingly in place during pauses. In cold water, when long pauses are mandatory, floating jerkbaits rise up out of the strike zone before bass have time to react.

"Today's production-line suspending jerkbaits are much improved," says Horton. "In the past, I had to fine-tune a lot of them by adding weight. Now I fish them right out of the package."

Thomas especially appreciates a suspending jerkbait when a bass approaches the lure but is reluctant to strike.

"I have better luck coaxing strikes from bass with a suspending jerkbait than with any other lure," says Thomas. "When you see the bass coming, you can hang the bait and practically work it in one spot until the bass strikes."

The Husky Jerks used by Patton are only available as suspending lures, which is just the way he likes it.

"Suspending jerkbaits cast better, especially under windy conditions," says Patton. "They also allow greater variation in the retrieve, so I can give the bass exactly what they want."

USE A DOWNSIZED jerkbait in clear water when the bass follow, but fail to strike, the larger models.

DOWNSIZE YOUR JERKBAITS ... DOUBLE YOUR CATCH

Bass anglers throughout the country are relying on little "jerks" for more action in clear water and tough bite situations

THE TACKLEBOXES of most accomplished bass anglers contain assorted jerkbaits from 4 1/2 to 5 1/2 inches in length. These lures cast well and draw bass from long distances, especially when worked with aggressive actions.

Some anglers also rely on diminutive jerkbaits, and these fishermen may not be eager to let you see their undersized lures. When bass turn up their noses or slap at standard jerkbaits, downsized jerkbaits can transform a frustrating day on the water into a heavy catch of bass.

Ohio BASS pro Frank Scalish once employed downsized jerkbaits while fishing a spring tournament on Kentucky Lake. During the first two days of the event, he keyed on main lake points leading into cuts, and on nearby gravel flats and shoals within the creeks. In the crystalline water, sizable smallmouth and largemouth bass shadowed Scalish's standard jerkbaits, but wouldn't nab them. When Scalish dropped to a 3 1/2-inch jerkbait, the bass inhaled the lure.

(Opposite page) FRANK SCALISH knows downsized jerkbaits can trigger strikes when bass refuse to look twice at standard jerkbaits.

"It rained overnight before the third day, which stained the water," says Scalish. "That killed the small jerkbait bite. But switching back to larger jerkbaits did the trick."

These days, Scalish usually starts with a downsized jerkbait in clear water, and he always drops in size when bass follow, but fail to strike, larger jerkbaits. His lure of choice is the suspending Pointer 78 from Lucky Craft Lures, one of a number of exquisitely finished jerkbaits made in Japan. While the Pointer 78 measures only 3 1/2 inches from the tail to the tip of its bill, Scalish claims it casts well for distance with a 6 1/2-foot 3-power (medium action) Falcon rod.

"The Pointer 78 runs about 5 feet deep on

Jerkbait Tip

Too often, anglers work jerkbaits in cold water just as they would in almost-perfect spawning conditions. To avoid this problem, use a rod with a soft tip and moderate backbone. The limber rod is more forgiving, allows for more subtle presentations, and really doesn't put the angler at a fighting disadvantage.

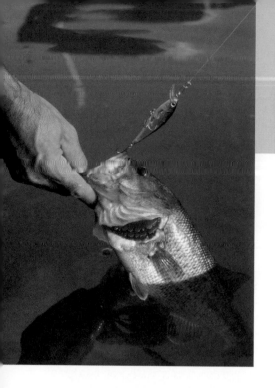

12-pound Silver Thread," says Scalish. "Lighter line stretches more, which hinders the bait's action, reduces hook setting efficiency and invites broken lines."

To increase the lure's wobbling action, Scalish always attaches a plain snap to the split ring that comes with the bait. The Pointer is designed with special brass weights that create a variable center of gravity. This makes the lure wobble and vibrate whenever the retrieve motion is stopped.

"When you pause the bait," says Scalish, "it continues to flutter a little bit."

Another reason small jerkbaits often do well is that they better match the size of the baitfish on which bass are feeding, such as threadfin shad. And when you match the lifelike eyes and finishes available on today's small jerkbaits, these realistic lures conjure a feeding bite.

"The finishes on many smaller jerkbaits are so natural," says Scalish, "bass see them as true baitfish. With a bigger jerkbait, they see the entire lure more clearly. Those lures are better for drawing bass from longer distances and triggering reflex strikes."

Scalish works downsized jerkbaits with more subdued actions to go along with their more subtle profiles. Instead of the snappy jerk-jerk-pause he imparts to large jerkbaits, Scalish sweeps small jerkbaits in short pulls that swim the lures ahead a foot at a time between pauses.

Almost all downsized jerkbaits come with two small trebles, as opposed to two or three bigger trebles found on larger jerkbaits. This appears to be a disadvantage in terms of landing fish, but bass tend to engulf the smaller jerkbaits deeper than larger models, making the lures more difficult to dis-

EXCALIBUR 3-INCH Minnows in floating, suspending and sinking models.

lodge. Combine this with a light hand when playing the bass, and you shouldn't lose many fish.

Owner, which is best known for its quality hooks, produces an extensive line of Cultiva Lures. Among these are two jerkbaits, the 2 3/5-inch, 1/4-ounce suspending Rip'n Minnow-65, and the 3 3/5-inch, 1/5-ounce floating Rip'n Minnow-90.

"These baits run 2 to 3 feet deep," says Owner's Dennis Yamamoto. "A lot of guys throw them when fishing waters that have threadfin shad. The lures have a seven-coat finish that combines foil with holographics. They also have internal rattles. The rattles in the RM65 rotate inside the bait for better casting and a level posture during the retrieve."

The treble hooks on these baits, points out Yamamoto, are specifically balanced to the lures. They are always perfectly positioned for hooking fish, and they don't offset the action of the little baits, which can be critical.

Smithwick offers a wide variety of popular downsized jerkbaits. One that especially appeals to perennial Top 150 angler Mark Menendez is the 3 1/2-inch, 1/4-ounce Rattlin' Rogue. This downsized version of its larger, legendary brothers features the same finishes and proven actions.

"The littlest Rogue dives 3 to 4 feet," says Menendez. "I throw it on a 6-foot glass TDX Team Daiwa rod with a 6.3:1 gear ratio Team Daiwa 103HVA baitcasting reel. That combination casts the light bait great. I spool the reel with 8- to 10-pound Triple Fish line."

Menendez ties on the little Rogue when he's confronted with clear water from prespawn through postspawn. He opts for chrome with a blue back in clear water and chrome with a black back and orange belly in slightly stained water.

When he fishes rivers, streams, creeks and ponds just for kicks, Menendez goes with the Rebel or Excalibur Ghost Minnow, a 2 1/4-inch jerkbait that weighs 1/9 ounce. His favorite color is silver with a gray back. These realistic baits catch about anything that feeds on baitfish, provided you fish the lures on light spinning tackle.

"If you don't go any heavier than 6- or 8-pound

Minijerkbaits At A Glance

Many more excellent downsized jerkbaits are available than those mentioned in this article. The following are others well worth considering.

Yo-Zuri's lifelike, floating Pin's Minnow has a transfer weight system and will catch anything that swims. It's available in a 2-inch, 1/16-ounce size, and also in a 2 3/4-, 1/8-ounce size. The smallest Yo-Zuri Suspending Crystal Minnow measures 3 5/8 inches. Its humpback profile features a luminescent finish and 3D eyes.

The XPS Lazer Eye Extreme Series baits from Bass Pro Shops includes the 2 3/4-inch LEMS floating minnow that weighs 1/8 ounce; the 3 1/2-inch, 3/16-ounce LEML floating; and the 3 1/2-inch LEM9F floater. All these lures are available in a variety of holographic finishes.

Rapala has a number of little jerkbaits, including its 3 1/2-inch, 3/16-ounce No. 9 floater; 2 3/4-inch, 1/8-ounce No. 7 floater; and the 2-inch, 1/16-ounce No. 5 floater. They also offer downsized Jointed Minnows, sinking Countdown Minnows and suspending Husky Jerks that have proved their bass catching ability.

ThunderSticks by Storm come in 2 1/2-inch, 1/8-ounce Baby; and 3 1/2-inch, 1/4-ounce Jr. sizes that perform admirably as downsized jerkbaits. The Deep Jr. ThunderStick, which measures 4 1/2 inches, also qualifies as a downsized jerkbait because it has essentially the same size body as the Jr. ThunderStick. The extra length is in the long bill.

Norman's 1/8-ounce, 2 1/2-inch Crappie Minner features a gelcoat finish and dives 6 feet on 6-pound line.

Luhr Jensen's Suspending Power Minnow measures 3 3/8 inches and has a wider belly than other downsized jerkbaits. It presents bass with a fatter profile when viewed from underneath. New photo and luminous finishes are available.

The Smithwick Super Rogue Junior is a 4 1/8-inch version of the popular Super Rogue. It features a built-in precision brass rattle chamber and is available in floating and suspending versions.

The new 3-inch Excalibur Minnow comes in floating, suspending and sinking models. These lures feature 3D eyes and "hyper-reflective" finishes.

---

line, the Ghost Minnow casts real well," says Menendez. "Anything over 10-pound test overpowers it. I either use a subsurface cadence retrieve, or I twitch it along as a surface bait. You never know what you're going to catch. Bluegill, crappie, little bass, big bass — just about anything will take a shot at it."

The 3 1/2-inch Bomber 14A gets kudos from Florida bass ace Bernie Schultz. He drops to this 1/4-ounce lure when he notices bass feeding on small forage, or whenever bass follow bigger jerkbaits but refuse to take them.

"I prefer Bombers that have the metallic inserts," says Schultz. "I especially like the one with the gold insert with a black back and orange belly, and the one with the chrome insert with the blue back. The inserts give the baits a realistic translucent look, and a lot of flash and a little extra weight, which make them cast better in the wind."

Schultz casts the Bomber 14A with baitcasting tackle and 10- to 12-pound-test Silver Thread. He switches to spinning gear when he fishes 2 1/2- and 3 1/2-inch Rebel Minnows, which he works by pulling them under and letting them float up to the surface.

"I generally go with the Rebel Minnow in clear water when bass are feeding on small baitfish near the surface," says Schultz. "I have my best luck with this tactic after the spawn, and on into the summer and fall. The periods when this bait works are brief, and they're generally related to low light conditions, such as morning, evening or around fronts. I work them along shorelines, over the tops of submerged grass, along the contours of topped out grass, and any place I see bass chasing minnows."

Before Schultz became involved in competitive fishing, small, jointed Rebels produced many bass for him. He has gotten away from these lures and plans to make amends.

"I used to catch a ton of bass on jointed Rebels, and I'm confident they'd still work great today," says Schultz. "I just have to force myself to fish them more, because I've seen situations where they made the difference."

BOMBER'S 14A (top), Smithwick's 3 1/2-inch Rattlin' Rogue.

JERKING FOR SPRINGTIME SMALLIES

Early season bronzebacks are suckers for a twitch bait. Learn where and how to work jerkbaits for spring smallmouth

ASKING PROFESSIONAL ANGLER Tim Horton to choose his favorite spring smallmouth bait is like asking a kid to choose between a dose of cough syrup and a piece of candy. The answer is easy.

"Jerkbaits," says the Alabama pro without a second's hesitation. "They are without a doubt my favorite spring smallmouth baits, and I'd say they are the most effective smallmouth bait this time of year."

The decision is just as simple for Rick Lillegard, a veteran tournament angler and guide from the smallmouth-rich state of New Hampshire. From the earliest days of New England's bass season and into summer and fall, the Lake Winnipesaukee guide keeps an Excalibur Suspending Rogue or a Bomber floating Long A rigged and ready to go.

"I don't throw them too much during the spawn itself because the bass are just too easy to catch when they are on their beds," he says. "I'll usually switch to a grub then."

As a former guide on northern Alabama's world-famous trophy smallmouth waters of Pickwick and Wilson lakes, Horton soon learned which lures put fish on his clients' lines and which ones didn't. As a tournament angler — both on his home waters and on great smallmouth waters throughout the country — he also figured out how to load up on quality smallmouth.

"A friend and I won a buddy tournament a few years back on Wilson Lake with 10 fish that weighed 37 pounds. They were all smallmouth, and they were all caught on jerkbaits. I'd say that without a doubt, more spring tournaments are won on jerkbaits on my home waters than on any other lure," he says.

Although Rogues, Long A's, Husky Jerks and an assortment of other makes and models will catch fish all year, both Horton and Lillegard get most excited about using them during the prespawn, spawn and postspawn periods. That's when smallmouth are most likely to hit one of these stickbaits as it darts and pauses through the water.

BASIC JERKING

For Horton, the prevailing water color is the determining factor for jerkbait color selection.

"If the water is clear to semistained, I know I'm going to catch smallmouth on jerkbaits. If the water is fairly dirty, however, I probably won't use a jerkbait. They definitely work best in clear water," says Horton.

In most northern and New England lakes, murky isn't a problem, so Lillegard rarely stashes his jerkbait box. But in the South, where feeder streams and rivers often resemble coffee-with-cream after a heavy spring rain, and lakes stay colored from algae growth, Horton has to decide what constitutes too much color.

"I like to be able to see at least 4 feet down," he adds. "The clearer the water, the better."

Where he starts fishing jerkbaits depends on the time of year, or more accurately, the stage of the spawn. Early in the season, Horton looks for such typical prespawn habitat as deeper secondary points and dropoffs adjacent to spawning flats. Lillegard targets sun-warmed coves with flats near shallow spawning areas and deeper ledges adjacent to spawning flats.

During the spawn, both experts hunt for bass in shallow coves, calm flats that receive plenty of afternoon sunshine, and other likely spawning areas. Find those areas, and you'll catch some nice bass.

A lure's ability to suspend is important during the prespawn phase, particularly when the water is in the low to high 50s. Smallmouth are less willing to chase a bait and won't expend much energy to eat it. For those reasons, Horton likes to put a Suspending Rogue in front of a smallmouth's nose and let it sit there a few seconds, and there's a real good chance the fish will eat it.

Spoonbilling For Smallies

In supercold water, Rick Lillegard uses a modified suspending jerkbait known as the Rebel Spoonbill.

"I'll use the Spoonbill when the water is between 38 and 45 degrees," he says. "I use a technique called ripping. It's real simple, and it accounts for some real nice stringers of smallmouth. It's not out of the question to catch 20 pounds with five fish."

The key is to throw the lure out as far as you can and then rip it back as hard as you can, pausing only as long as it takes to wind up the slack. Sweep the rod hard, reel in the slack and sweep it hard again. The length of the pause only needs to be a couple of seconds, but Lillegard will experiment with different lengths to see what the fish want.

"The bass will be suspended about 10 or 15 feet down, and the lure gets down about 8 feet on 10-pound Silver Thread, so the fish aren't moving far to hit the bait," he notes. "If you stay warm on a cold day, then you know you're doing this technique right. It can be a real workout."

Lillegard rips suspending Rebel Spoonbills along rock bluff walls and in quiet coves that receive direct sunlight throughout the day. Those sun-warmed coves tend to attract bass seeking a few degrees of extra heat.

Jerkbait Tip

Follow the natural life cycle of the real minnow when choosing jerkbait size. Use smaller baits early in the year, when shad fry and other forage are typically smaller. Progressively increase the size of the chosen jerkbait into the summer and fall.

INDEX